21
Twenty
One

21
Designers
for
twenty-
first
century
Britain

21 Twenty One

21 Designers for twenty-first century Britain

Gareth Williams

V&A Publishing

First published by V&A Publishing, 2012
Victoria and Albert Museum
South Kensington
London SW7 2RL
www.vandabooks.com

Distributed in North America by Harry N. Abrams Inc.,
New York

ISBN 978 1 85177 678 8

Library of Congress Control Number 2011935106

10 9 8 7 6 5 4 3 2 1
2016 2015 2014 2013 2012

A catalogue record for this book is available from
the British Library.

Front and back cover illustration:
Martino Gamper / A Practice for Everyday Life

Design:
A Practice for Everyday Life

Printed in China

V&A Publishing

Supporting the world's leading
museum of art and design,
the Victoria and Albert
Museum, London

Photographic credits

All portraits by Petr Krejčí, except for Jaime Hayon,
page 95, by Nienke Klunder.

Fig.1: © Alex Eckford; fig.2: Dennis Gilbert/VIEW;
fig.3: Courtesy of Urban Salon Ltd; fig.4: Photo
by Iwan Baan courtesy of Heatherwick Studio;
fig.5: Photos by Jung Jin Kyu, courtesy of the British
Council, except Import/Export (above, right),
© The Victoria and Albert Museum, London;
fig.6: Photo by Miguel Angel Blanco; fig.7: Royal
College of Art; figs 8–9: Photos by El Ultimo Grito;
fig.10: © Photos by Mike Golgwater; fig.11: Courtesy
Raw Edges; fig.22: Photos by Emma Wieslander;
fig.25: Photo by Beppe Brancato; figs 26–8:
Photos by Industrial Facility; fig.29: Photo by Peter
Guenzel; fig.30: Photo by Industrial Facility; fig.31:
Photo by Angela Moore; fig.32: © Meta; fig.33:
© Established & Sons; figs 34 and 36: © Thorsten van
Elten; fig.35: Photo by André Klauser; figs 37–40:
© 2011 Doshi Levien; figs 41–2: Photos by Peter
Guenzel; figs 43–4: Courtesy David Gill Gallery;
fig.50: © Troika; fig.51: © Alex Delfanne / Artwise
Curators; fig.52 © Michelle Sadgrove; fig.53:
Courtesy of Rachel Verghis / Incubator, photography
© by rAndom International; fig.54: Courtesy of
Carpenters Workshop Gallery, photography
© by rAndom International; fig.55: Courtesy
of The Victoria and Albert Museum, London /
Carpenters Workshop Gallery, photography
© by rAndom International; fig.60: Photo by Philip
Sinden; figs 61–4: All photos © Studio Simon Heijdens
Ltd, fig.63: Photo by Gideon Hart, courtesy Gallery
Libby Sellers; fig.65: Photos by Sylvain Deleu; fig.67:
Photos on page 138 by Diego Trujillo (page 139
© The Victoria and Albert Museum, London);
fig.69: Photo by Gideon Hart, courtesy Gallery
Libby Sellers; fig.71: Photo © Fabrice Gousset,
courtesy Galerie Kreo; fig.72: Photo by Julia
Lohmann; fig.73: Photo by Amendolagine
Barracchia, courtesy Galleria Nilufar; fig.74:
Courtesy Stanley Picker Gallery, Kingston University.
Photo: ellielaycock.co.uk; fig.76: Photo by Petr
Krejčí; figs 81–2: Photos by Thomas Brown; fig.83:
Photos by Fredrikson Stallard; fig.84: Photo by
Angus Mill; figs 85–6: Courtesy Galleria Nilufar,
Milan; fig.87: Photos © Courtesy of Flos; fig.88:
Photos © Richard Brine; fig.89: Photos © Courtesy
of Swarovski Crystal Palace collection and Mark
Cocksedge; fig.90: Photos © Richard Brine; fig.91:
Photos © Mark Cocksedge; fig.92: Photo by Nic
Ballon; figs 95–6: Photo by Nick Mora

Contents

Foreword
Tord Boontje

The content of design today has shifted significantly compared to the decades before 2000. Design was seen as an activity primarily concerned with making products more efficient to manufacture, more efficient to use and prettier to look at. Important terms in the designer's lexicon were 'integration of parts', 'ergonomics' and 'lifestyle'. For sure, there is still a part of design that addresses 'brand value', 'competitiveness' and 'markets', but few or none of the designers featured in this book would place great significance on such words. If we compare their practices to what came before we are reminded of artists, inventors, poets and performers. Their activities have very little to do with 'styling' and 'marketing'; their interest is much more centred on innovation, narrative, expression and experience.

I think there are three focuses that are significant to design today:
- Extreme Functionality: the optimum performance of products in their use and creation.
- The Social Manifesto: design that can improve daily life for all people and our environment.
- The Fantastic: design that can enrich our personal wellbeing.

These are not separate areas or design disciplines; they overlap. I see these focuses as tools with which students can analyse their work and understand their own position in the world.

The 21 designers featured here have a strong affinity with the notion of the Fantastic, although they are very aware of the other two focuses as well. However, I also see a shift in current design students, who place much more emphasis on social issues. This tells me that the definition of design has not come to rest, but is still evolving. The next generation, as well as the people in this book, have taken the liberty to create work that is meaningful to themselves and hopefully to a larger audience. In doing so, they are redefining what design is.

This book, compiled by Gareth Williams with great care and thought, is a beautiful reflection on a very exciting part of design today. It presents an inspiring collection of people, who are all, in different ways, committed to making our world a little bit more wonderful.

21 Designers for twenty-first century Britain: Design as Cultural Diplomacy

Gareth Williams

This book presents a selection of designers living and working in Britain who have come to prominence since the millennium; but the definition needs some qualification. Those selected represent a certain way of being a designer: they lead critical debate and regard design as a cultural activity; they are the innovators and the explorers of new materials and processes, and of different ways of working, even of new definitions of design itself.

Design practice is so diverse that it is not possible to cover all its permutations in a book of this size. The focus here is on designers of furniture and products, who design for industrial production, or whose practice relates to product design, even if they now work more for galleries than for the mass market. This is not a compendium of designers in all disciplines. Undoubtedly Britain is a leading centre for communication design, including all forms of graphics, branding, packaging, advertising and digital design. Speaking in terms of the whole design industry, communications is Britain's biggest sector and its proponents are well represented in print elsewhere. The stars of British fashion and architecture are also celebrated internationally, with vast literatures of their own, and British expertise in specialisms such as vehicle design and computer games is widely recognized. I have chosen my focus not because I think the furniture and product design sector is more interesting, but because it is the area of design with which I am most involved.

Many (though not all) of the designers included here are associated with the Royal College of Art in London, either as graduates or tutors of the Design Products programme for which I also teach. As the only entirely postgraduate art and design college in the world, the Royal College of Art naturally attracts many of the brightest and most innovative student designers, who quickly gain prominence.

This selection opens with the most established studio, El Ultimo Grito, founded in 1997. Several of the designers who follow studied with Roberto Feo at the Royal College of Art, including Peter Marigold and Raw Edges, who appear alongside near peers Max Lamb and Simon Hasan. These are also designers with similar career trajectories through the patronage of Design Miami/Basel and clients such as Fendi.

A group of the designers included here – Industrial Facility, Doshi Levien, Klauser and Carpenter and Alexander Taylor – represent industrial and furniture design with a more commercial focus. Jaime Hayon is also resolutely commercial, but has a hybrid practice whereby his work can be seen simultaneously on the shelves of shops, in galleries and as branding. Troika, rAndom International, Moritz Waldemeyer and Simon Heijdens engage with the digital realm rather than designing tangible products for the mass market. To a lesser or greater degree the remaining designers act like artists, or are artists who engage with design.

I have asked four participants – El Ultimo Grito, Troika, Julia Lohmann and Fredrikson Stallard – to respond to some questions about their practices. These are provocations intended to elicit more information or clarity about their various positions. Both El Ultimo Grito and Troika have published widely before, so this is a chance for some specific, and I hope, penetrating insight. For Julia Lohmann and Fredrikson Stallard, it is an opportunity for us to hear the opinions of less frequently published designers. The photographer Petr Krejčí has contributed specially commissioned photographs of the designers in their studios, to give us a sense of the spaces where they work.

I have described these designers as innovators and explorers, and leaders of taste and critical debate. Fascinatingly, many of them share another characteristic, which is more a role imposed on them than one they have chosen. In various ways they are agents of cultural diplomacy, where contemporary design – especially highly characterful and visible design – has become entwined with a sense of Britishness. In the twenty-first century social, political and economic policy have co-opted design and designers to signal or engender change in a way that has both exploited and promoted the interests of the designers themselves.

Although their work will be well known to followers of the design media, they are not yet household names like some fashion designers or architects. Rather than simply describing their works to build a 'greatest hits' list of objects or projects, I have tried to focus on the designers themselves. The main reason for choosing these particular designers was because they have already gained a critical head of steam, even though many of them are still in the first decade of their careers. Most of them have won national or international recognition in the form of prizes, honours and residencies, from the design media and at international events. Some of them have held solo exhibitions, and most have had their work exhibited in prestigious museums or acquired for permanent collections. These are the criteria I used for selecting people for this book, but doubtless there are other designers who could have been featured in these pages.

With very many different priorities, personal agendas, aesthetics and ambitions, just about the only consistent link between the people included here is that they reside in Britain. If you were one of these designers, what would you be like? Design Council research has revealed that the average designer in Britain is 38 years old, white and male (like Ian Stallard).[1] But it is quite likely that you were not born in the UK (like 20 of the designers profiled in this book). Deyan Sudjic has written of the British education system 'which, at least until recently, has been a kind of state-licensed archipelago of dissent, in the shape of the art school tradition', so possibly you are European and came to Britain to take advantage of Britain's art school training, choosing to stay after graduation (for example Patrik Fredrikson or Julia Lohmann).[2] It is likely you have settled in London, home to a quarter of all UK design businesses.[3] Perhaps it was London's hybrid and multinational character, or the network of other designers and creatives who live there, that attracted you (Jaime Hayon, Moritz Waldemeyer). Quite probably you chose to set up your own studio, or to create a new practice with your former college mates (Glithero, Troika). You aspire to generate your own projects, priding yourself on your independent thought and quirky signature style, both of which result from your robust British design education (Paul Cocksedge, Simon Hasan). If you are lucky this singular vision will have led to an invitation to take part in a British Council touring exhibition celebrating the creativity of young British designers (Committee, Doshi Levien). A sign of increasing success is when one of the major design fairs such as the London Design Festival or Design Miami/Basel commission an installation or an event, or give you a prize (Max Lamb, Peter Marigold, Raw Edges). Maybe an auction house has courted you for your early prototypes, or a museum has included your work in a survey exhibition (Martino Gamper). A prominent design-led manufacturer like Swarovski or Established & Sons, or one of the Italian companies such as Moroso may have produced your work, either as a one-off exhibition piece or, better still, as a genuinely mass-produced product (Industrial Facility, Klauser and Carpenter, Alexander Taylor). Or it could have been one of the design galleries like the Carpenters Workshop Gallery or Gallery Libby Sellers who helped you promote yourself to a wider audience (Simon Heijdens, rAndom International). You might even have curated your own museum exhibitions (El Ultimo Grito, Onkar Kular and Noam Toran). About 10 or 15 years out of college, you are young enough still to be a fresh 'young designer' but old enough to have a rich portfolio of commissions and personal projects. Yet it is also quite likely that you are earning little, despite the wealth of international projects in your portfolio, and that you supplement your studio with a bit of teaching. All or some of these events or situations characterize the designers in this book.

It is notable that none of these people are employed by a large corporation or consultancy; they prefer to remain independent or, at most, work together collectively. In the 1980s and 1990s British design would have been distinguished more by consultancies such as IDEO, Tangerine or Seymourpowell. Since 2000 few consultancies have arisen to match these in scale. Now, more established product designers like Pearson Lloyd (led by Luke Pearson and Tom Lloyd), BarberOsgerby (Ed Barber and Jay Osgerby) and Tord Boontje maintain relatively small and tightly focused studios. Possibly this shift away from larger consultancies towards independent operators signals a growing confidence among the younger generation of designers to 'go it alone'. Conversely it may indicate fragmentation or a decline in the sector, and certainly the presence of more freelancers indicates tighter corporate budgets squeezing in-house design team numbers and consultancy headcounts.[4] Freelance designers, design consultancies and in-house design teams each represent roughly a third of all designers in the UK, of which there are reportedly some 232,000, an increase of 29 per cent since 2005.[5] While the designers in this book are largely atypical of their profession because of their independence, role models like Ron Arad and Tom Dixon showed the way for younger designers to work outside large companies. In another way, they are completely typical of the British design profession, where 87 per cent of consultancies work in very small teams and employ fewer than 10 staff.[6] Small studios may be nimble and autonomous, but they are also financially exposed and vulnerable to market pressures. Increasingly, emerging designers are coalescing into informal collectives where they can share spaces and resources.

Stepping back from the particular experiences of designers living in Britain, I would like to consider how design has been perceived in the UK over the last 10 or 15 years, to give a context for the designers discussed in detail in this book. Design in Britain has a venerable history, and a rich present. Britain claims many design 'firsts', not least as the cradle of the Industrial Revolution in the eighteenth century, and arguably the most enduring legacy of the Great Exhibition in 1851 was that it gave Britain 'ownership' of industrial design on the world stage.[7] In many ways it could be argued that Britain still has this ownership of design, alongside powerhouses like Japan, Italy and Germany, but the terms of its propriety have changed. For a start, notions of nationalism have been transformed,

and for a long time it has not been possible to talk about 'British design', only 'design in Britain'. More than ever Britain is a multicultural society, and despite marginal political or local opposition, it continues to welcome immigrants. Moreover, London lays claim to be a 'world city' with residents originating from all corners of the globe: a tolerant international hub for the exchange of ideas, where from time to time cultures may clash, but where internationalism generally benefits all. This internationalism directly affects design, and as Deyan Sudjic points out, a characteristic of designers in Britain is that 'they are British by choice rather than birth'.[8] To demonstrate this point, of the 34 people who make up the 21 design studios in this book, only 14 were born in Britain.

Making a national identity is an act of conscious creation – of designing – and the relationship between design and notions of Britishness reappears through this book. Deyan Sudjic notes that 'national identity is itself a carefully constructed artefact, dependent on a wide range of self-conscious design skills, rather than the organic and inevitable outcome of race memory or national temperament'.[9]

1. (*opposite, left*)
British Airways installation, 2000
Millennium Dome, London

2. (*opposite, right*)
Millennium Products
exhibition installation by
Conran Design Group, 2000
Centre for Contemporary Art,
Ujazdowski Castle, Warsaw

The big question is when and how did contemporary designers become part of Britain's self-image? In the 18 years of Tory rule from 1979 (a conservative era with both a big and small 'c') national identity was generally associated with notions of heritage, and historic Britain was the leitmotif for promoting Britain abroad (using anything from the Royal House of Windsor to the televised 'House of Eliott', a period drama aired from 1991 to 1994). Around 1995, under the Conservative Minister for National Heritage, Virginia Bottomley, a new spirit began to emerge that sought to associate Britishness with up-to-date innovation, coalescing under the punning term 'Cool Britannia'. By the final years of John Major's government the Millennium Dome had been commissioned and the stage was set for the incoming New Labour regime to co-opt design – and designers – to its grand new project, nothing less than rebranding Britain itself (fig.1).

Delivered to Downing Street on the very first day of Tony Blair's tenure in May 1997, the report *Britain™: Renewing Our Identity* was published jointly by the think-tank Demos and the Design Council. It trumpeted the case for rebranding Britain and its national identity, both consciously to reject the recent Conservative past and to further the social, economic and idealistic ambitions of New Labour. Design (with all the creative industries) was central to this scheme. Writing in the paperback version that appeared later that year, its author, Mark Leonard, attempted to gather the zeitgeist to his cause: 'Renewed confidence in the arts, fashion, technology, architecture and design has coincided with the departure from Hong Kong, devolution, further integration with Europe, the imminence of the millennium and Princess Diana's death.'[10]

On inspection, in some ways the ambitions of *Britain™* came to pass. The report found that the key to recasting the nation's identity should be to emphasize 'Britain's place as a hub, an importer and exporter of ideas, goods and services, people and cultures'.[11] Britain is indeed a centre or intersection where people exchange ideas and trade (underpinning the cultural benefits with real economic gains). In addition, the report recognized and celebrated 'Britain's history as a hybrid nation' and 'our traditions of creativity and non-conformism'. All this is evident in the strong design scene in Britain today.

The report also noted that while British manufacturing and design were broadly respected abroad, they were perceived as rather safe and dull, yet the reality was that design had never been so innovative and active. The answer was for the nation to exploit its contemporary designers as ambassadors, for example to redesign the points of entry to the UK to 'provide visitors with a stunning welcome to the country', a call largely borne out with the building of Terminal 5 at Heathrow Airport and the redevelopment of St Pancras Station in London as an international rail hub.[12] (While the former employed the talents of Troika and others, the latter went somewhat off-message with Paul Day's sculpture *The Meeting Place*.) At the heart of the report was a call to replace the old, dated ideas that informed Britishness with new stories to shape national identity. Britain is a creative and individualistic island: 'We have a history of eccentricity and quirkiness, and an ethos that values individuality, non-conformity, new ideas and difference … Cultivating that creativity requires us to remain a diverse, challenging society; resisting pressures to conformity; valuing the new even if it is disturbing; and seeing creative fields not as marginal but as central to our economic future.'[13] Britain's multiculturalism, tradition of trade (as a 'nation of shopkeepers'), social innovation and sense of fair play may seem to be more conventional British values, but the report used examples that were a far cry from John Major's 'warm beer and cricket' vision for the nation that they superseded. Finally *Britain™* called, somewhat chillingly, for 'identity control' to be centralized in the Cabinet Office and renewed its appeal for the creation of a cadre of design and creative ambassadors. The impending millennium would be the focus of presenting this new, modern, creative Britain, and the celebrations should focus on international outreach because (in a singular moment of massive understatement) 'for a country with as distinctive a military history as Britain it is not surprising that our relations with other countries are not as good as they could be'.[14]

Looking back some 15 years, it is sometimes hard to remember the euphoria that accompanied the arrival of Tony Blair's New Labour government in 1997, but Stephen Bayley's often acid recollections of the planning for the Millennium Dome in Greenwich, *Labour Camp*, remind us how far government imagery was substituted for actual policy (or, as he put it, the failure of style over substance). It appeared that design had reached the top table of influence, and designers were certainly feted, commissioned, published and promoted. But in fact the design industry was being used as a tool to promote an image of New Labour, and by extension its image of a new Britain. Stephen Bayley regards himself as something of a design guru, so felt well qualified to point out New Labour's design failings. 'Cool Britannia is a fundamental misunderstanding of the relationship between product and brand. Genuine brand value depends on substance, on associations and expectations over time', he wrote. 'In that it's a lazy cliché which evokes a rather dopey concept of style, it is characteristic of a Camp regime which insists on appearance over substance.' If you accept his version of events 'Cool Britannia mugged the intellectuals'.[15]

Bayley, the founding director of the Design Museum in London, had been appointed as Creative Director for the Millennium Dome in 1997 but rapidly fell foul of New Labour politicians who, he claimed, had no clear idea about the content of the new attraction, and by the following year he had left the project. By his own admission he wanted to 'do an 1851' with the Dome, declaring that the success of the Great Exhibition had been to claim 'symbolic ownership' of industrial design by Britain. Bayley had high ambitions for the Dome: 'I believe that the Millennium Experience should be an elegant and economical exhibition about the world of the future, designed by the greatest architects and designers available: accessible to the public, comprehensible to the media and with technical collaboration from the world's greatest industries who would be involved as creative partners, not arm's-length sponsors.'[16] To a large extent this is what the project delivered, with input from big-name designers and architects (not least Lord Rogers, whose architectural practice designed the Dome itself), but chronic budget over-runs and intrusive sponsorship fatally dulled the event. At the end of *Labour Camp* Bayley wrote an open letter to Tony Blair outlining his vision for the Dome. Although it is all about the future, in retrospect Bayley's ambitions were quotidian and lacklustre: 'Ford would show us the car of the future, Sainsbury's the shop of the future, Microsoft the library of the future, while Guinness would explain if we are still going to be using pubs (or even actually drinking) in 2051.'[17]

The Dome was far from the only attempt to harness politics to design and creativity. Launched in 1998, the Creative Industries Task Force appeared to be the cadre of creative ambassadors envisaged in *Britain™*. It comprised fashion designer Paul Smith, Gail Rebuck (the CEO of publisher Random House) and Richard Branson, among others, and was a joint venture by numerous Whitehall departments, including the DCMS (Department for Culture, Media and Sport), the DTI (Department of Trade and Industry), the Treasury and the Foreign Office, as well as Education and Employment. It was led by the Culture Secretary, Chris Smith, who had commissioned the first research into the economic benefits to the nation of the so-called 'creative industries'. Smith had concluded that these industries, which included all forms of design alongside pop music, fashion, film, computer software and advertising, created some 50,000 jobs and £60bn of revenues in the previous year alone. Although largely unquantifiable Smith's statistics made a strong case for the economic, if not the cultural, importance of design for the health of Britain.

It was clear that design was a beneficiary of the National Lottery, launched by the Conservative government in 1994, when Smith announced the foundation of NESTA (the National Endowment for Science, Technology and the Arts) in 1998, endowed with £200m of lottery cash. He described NESTA as 'a National Trust for talent', and defined its threefold aims as nurturing talent, turning creativity into products and advancing the public appreciation of the creative industries.[18] Smith, regarded as one of the more serious arts ministers in recent times, nevertheless opened himself to ridicule (not least by Stephen Bayley) by publishing various speeches and policy launches together as *Creative Britain* in 1998. Seen together they are a blatant attempt to gain political capital from creative endeavour, as were Tony Blair's infamous Downing Street soirées where he mixed with rock stars and fashion designers. NESTA sponsored a project proposed by John Sorrell, Head of the Design Council, to find 1,000 British products to celebrate the year 2000, packaging them all in a quasi-New Labour brand as 'Millennium Products' (fig.2). In truth there were far fewer products of merit available and the pickings remained thin. Despite a global tour by the British Council, the project has not stood the test of time, in contrast to the Design Council's awards from some 40 years previously.

In 1998 the DTI commissioned an exhibition about the creative industries, to take place in a pavilion designed by Nigel Coates placed on Horse Guards Parade in the heart of Whitehall. The exhibition curator, Claire Catterall, linked the sensibilities of designers to the particularities of British national identity, writing, 'It is the great British tradition of non-conformity, individualism and courage that makes us different. We're a nation made up of inventors, iconoclasts and romantic dreamers.'[19] Muscularly entitled *Powerhouse::uk*, the exhibition was a showcase for recent work by designers including Jasper Morrison, Michael Marriott, Tord Boontje, Inflate and Tom Dixon. Design, endorsed by government, was seen to represent the British national spirit. Catterall followed up with the exhibition *Stealing Beauty: British Design Now*, held at the ICA in the spring of 1999 (fig.3). This was one of the first celebrations of this generation of designers in a major British cultural institution and included many of the designers from her previous show together with Dunne & Raby, Michael Anastassiades, Georg Baldele, MUF, Bump, Alex Rich and El Ultimo Grito, among others. Catterall declared these were 'designers who are searching for a new method and meaning in design'. They were less interested in designing the clunking political trophies of New Labour's Millennium Products, than in redefining design as a creative process. This was design in the service of culture, rather than politics, and set the tone for the subsequent decade. These and other exhibitions, for example those in Glasgow for the Year of Architecture in 1999, for the Jerwood Applied Arts prizes and at the V&A, heralded the ways in which design would be embraced as a cultural force in the twenty-first century. The various iterations of an annual Brit Insurance Designs of the Year exhibition at the Design Museum since 2008, with television coverage from Channel 4, has further served to promote and embed contemporary design in the

3.
Stealing Beauty: British Design Now exhibition installation, 1999 Institute for the Contemporary Arts, London

British public consciousness. Exhibitions like *Wouldn't it be Nice… Wishful Thinking in Art and Design*, at Somerset House in London (2008), emphasized design's cultural capacity. Most notably, it was the development of cultural diplomacy using design as an ambassador for Britain that has shaped and promoted much leading edge design practice in this century.

Joseph Nye, the Professor of International Relations at Harvard University, describes cultural diplomacy as 'a prime example of "soft power" or the ability to persuade through culture, value'. This is opposed to what he describes as 'hard power', which coerces through military might, economic sanctions or espionage.[20] Design can be variously described as the quest for solutions and as communication, so maybe it naturally lends itself to cultural diplomacy. 'As identity politics exert an increasing influence on domestic and international exchanges, culture

is therefore a critical forum for negotiation and a medium of exchange in finding shared solutions', stated Demos in its report on cultural diplomacy. It continued:

> Cultural contact provides a forum for unofficial political relationship-building: it keeps open negotiating channels with countries where political connections are in jeopardy, and helps to recalibrate relationships for changing times with emerging powers such as India and China. In the future, alliances are just as likely to be forged along lines of cultural understanding as they are on economic or geographic ones. However, culture should not be used as a tool of public diplomacy. The value of cultural activity comes precisely from its independence, its freedom and the fact that it represents and connects people, rather than necessarily governments or policy positions. Cultural institutions and others in the cultural sector must not only retain their independence, but also be brought more into the policy-making process.[21]

4. (*opposite*)
Seed Cathedral installation
by Heatherwick Studio, 2010
Shanghai World Expo

When *Britain™* called for a redesign of the ports of entry into the UK, using contemporary design to signal a contemporary nation, it was proposing design in the service of cultural diplomacy. Back in 1998 an Anglo-French summit was controversially staged in a suite high up in the Canary Wharf tower at One Canada Square, rather than in conventional Whitehall. Sir Terence Conran was drafted in to supervise (or, at least, to endorse) the sleek modern furnishings. One suspects this example of cultural diplomacy, in a temporary stage set with borrowed furniture, was somewhat lost on the French, who had been commissioning cutting edge interiors for the Elysée Palace for years. It could also be that the event fell at the first hurdle, because design and culture were too obviously co-opted, losing their independence and therefore their vitality.

Since the millennium we have seen more confident and successful examples of Britain designing and building a new image for itself on the international stage, for example the celebrated British Embassy in Berlin by Michael Wilford and Partners (2000). International expositions have always provided opportunities for national promotion (if not their principle purpose). In 1992 the cool restraint of Nicholas Grimshaw's high-tech architecture represented Britain at the Seville Expo, but by the time of the Shanghai World Expo in 2010 nothing less than a grand and flamboyant gesture would suffice. In the most expensive international exhibition ever staged, Thomas Heatherwick's exuberant 'Seed Cathedral' was among the most popular, and most visited of the pavilions, surely making him Britain's de facto 'cultural diplomat' (fig.4). Neither did the project harm Troika, the young multi-disciplinary practice that supplied some of the pavilion's content. Of course, to an extent embassy-building and world's fair pavilions are ego-boosts for nations anxious to let others know they are still there and still count. This is as important for nations gaining international significance as it is for those, like Britain, whose status on the world stage is in decline. Hosting the Olympic Games is a perfect opportunity for nations to present themselves favourably, and designers create and enhance the setting against which the athletes perform. BarberOsgerby's torch and Thomas Heatherwick's cauldron may well come to represent the London 2012 games as much as buildings such as Zaha Hadid's Aquatics Centre.

Arguably during the first decade of the new millennium it was the British Council that did most to promote contemporary designers on the world stage. The British Council was formed in 1934 with a remit to foster friendship and understanding between Britain and other nations through education and culture. Today it is a major supplier of English language teaching and qualifications overseas, and continues to promote an agenda of cultural diplomacy. Design used to be part of what was called 'commercial art' so it offered both cultural and tangible

5. (*opposite*)
British Council exhibition
installations, *Import Export*,
2005 The Victoria and Albert
Museum, London (*above,
right*) and *Great Brits:
Ingenious Therapies*, 2007
Paul Smith, Milan

commercial benefits to the nation. It was not until the late 1990s, however, that the British Council fully engaged with contemporary design as a tool for cultural diplomacy. In 1996 the Royal Society of Arts, the Design Council, the Department of Trade and Industry and the British Council together commissioned a report about the potential for design to play a larger cultural and diplomatic role, preceding *Britain™* by a year. *Excellence in Design* was commissioned with the express aim to 'promote Britain's design skills internationally to enhance Britain's image as a forward-looking, innovative and creative society'.[22] The initiative led directly to the creation of a new role of 'Promoting Britain Worldwide Through Design Officer' within the British Council. Very quickly the appointee, Emily Campbell, was in control of an Architecture and Design department and was determined to showcase the best practice emerging from Britain. Funded directly by the Foreign Office, it was evident that all the British Council's activities should pertain to Britain's reputation and reception overseas, yet Campbell did not see her role as simply an advocate for British design. Rather, she aspired to being a design critic who could present best practice on the world stage, either to celebrate Britain's ability to nurture talent, or as inspiration for designers in the host cities for the numerous exhibitions her department toured.[23]

The internationalism of many British Council exhibitions is of note. Campbell and her team realized that it was not possible simply to broadcast the message that 'Britain is great', and the exhibitions almost always sought two-way dialogue to promote understanding between Britain and other nations. Even where a degree of jingoism was to be expected, for example three exhibitions called *Great Brits* staged in Milan during successive furniture fairs, the selection always included at least one Dutch designer, and was more about the people for whom Britain had provided opportunities than about any notions of Britishness and design. *Import Export* (2003, see fig.5), examined the internationalism of designers based in Britain, including Tord Boontje, the jeweller Lara Bohinc, Gitta Gschwendtner, and Shin and Tomoko Azumi. 'Not since the wave of émigrés fleeing Nazi Germany in the 1930s has British design had such an injection of foreign blood', wrote Emily Campbell in the catalogue.[24] The curator, Lesley Jackson, asked the designers in the exhibition why they choose to come here. They answered that it was the quality of British design education and the access to an international design network that drew them.[25] In each international venue the exhibition expanded to include a section about local designers, making it the site of a genuine interchange of ideas. In 2007 the British Council followed up with *The New World*, an exhibition of six designers from countries outside the conventional design world, presented during the London Design Festival to a British design audience. The exhibition included representatives from Slovenia, South

Africa, Mexico, Brazil and India, none of whom were based in the UK. Many of the designers in this book have benefited from exposure on the international stage through British Council exhibitions.

The heady days of New Labour, *Britain™*, *Creative Britain* and the Dome were short-lived, banished by the 9/11 attacks and the subsequent political climate. In 2001 the Design Council sponsored an exhibition of British design called *Great Expectations* that took place in Grand Central Station, New York and then toured North America, China, Japan and Australia. It was planned before, but staged in the aftermath of 9/11, which transformed it from a trade exercise to promote exports to a symbolic act of support for an ally. Emily Campbell recalled that the British Council's exhibition agenda focused wholly on cultural diplomacy after 9/11, losing any pretence of being about promoting British exports. As the 2000s drew on, with economic and political clouds gathering around Labour (now no longer 'New'), state engagement with design and the creative industries waned. By 2011 the government, by now a Conservative and Liberal Democrat coalition, was still speaking enthusiastically about design, even if policy support was less forthcoming. In March that year Chancellor George Osborne concluded his budget speech with these (hollow) sentiments:

> We want the words:
> 'Made in Britain'
> 'Created in Britain'
> 'Designed in Britain'
> 'Invented in Britain'
> To drive our nation forward. A Britain carried aloft by the march of the makers. That is how we will create jobs and support families. We have put fuel into the tank of the British economy, and I commend this Budget to the House.[26]

Yet, while lacking state support, it is not true that design was without powerful patrons. One of the most significant initiatives of the Design Council, with the Sorrell Foundation, was the 'Joined up Design for Schools' initiative, piloted in 2000 and expanded thereafter, that gave pupils the role of client for a design project at their school, at a time of unprecedented expenditure on the infrastructure of education. The London Design Festival, founded in 2003 and funded by the London Development Agency, the Arts Council and private sponsorship, seeks to be both cultural and commercial. By celebrating the diversity and internationalism of design in London, to both a national and international audience, the festival's aims are in absolute accord with *Britain™*. It acts as an umbrella for several hundred events and exhibitions taking place each September, and initiates a few high-profile projects of its own. These include an annual London Design Medal awarded to a luminary (for example Thomas Heatherwick in 2010, and Ron Arad in 2011), and conspicuous sculptural installations around the Southbank Centre and Trafalgar Square, both significant cultural and civic landmarks for London and the nation. Several designers in this book, among them Fredrikson Stallard, Jaime Hayon and Paul Cocksedge, have benefited from the exposure afforded by these commissions, as have architects including Amanda Levete, Zaha Hadid and David Adjaye.

Through their funding, the Design Council and the London Design Festival still represent state investment in design, but there have also been other revenue streams. The Wellcome Trust, a wealthy medical charity based in London, has actively patronized designers including Julia Lohmann, Doshi Levien and Paul Cocksedge, who have contributed content for its public-facing programme of window displays. Internationally, many designers in this book have been commissioned by the Austrian crystal manufacturer Swarovski, which has emerged, since 2002, as a major patron of luxury design. In 2005 Britain gained a prominent high-end design manufacturer in the form of Established & Sons, the kind of maverick, independent company that many observers have seen as characteristic of design in Britain, which seeks to compete with big Italian brands on their own Milanese home turf (and which has employed many of the designers in this book, among them Klauser and Carpenter and Raw Edges).

Mass production is not morally superior to one-off production for galleries or self-initiated or self-made work, it is simply that it has the potential to reach larger audiences. Established & Sons is the type of client many designers aspire to gain: a design-led manufacturer of high-quality volume products. Yet relative to the entire spectrum of production, the firm's volumes are tiny. Of all the designers discussed here Industrial Facility are most engaged with mass production, but even their work with Muji, effectively a boutique retailer rather than a high-street mass-market store, does not take them into the mainstream. While mass-market manufacturing fails to exploit designers' talents it is unsurprising that they should seek other outlets, such as galleries and commissioned work.

Later in this book Julia Lohmann writes about materials becoming words and design as syntax, and we discuss the confluence of design and language as a means of communication. Lohmann is not really concerned with designing products for mass production, but is eager to communicate her design ideas. Therefore galleries, museums and exhibitions give her a platform in relatively safe isolation from commercial constraints. It is with some irony, however, that the principle significance of many of her designs is that they can be related back to the world of mass production, and to our husbandry of natural resources. She is a powerful critical voice in design, but her ideas could be more potent if they left the academy and influenced industry. Perhaps the same could be argued for Max Lamb, Martino Gamper, Glithero and other designers who work at the gallery end of the design spectrum.

Gallery projects can also lead designers into the world of commercial patronage, 'design art' and prizes, for example the Design Museum's Brit Insurance Designs of the Year award, Design Miami/Basel Designers of the Future awards, or the page-filling annual awards by magazines such as *Wallpaper** and *Elle Decoration*. While design awards are flattering to the recipient, it should not be forgotten that awards principally exist to aggrandize the awarding corporation or institution and their sponsors, and in this sense can be seen as another example, alongside state-sponsored cultural diplomacy, of the appropriation of designers' abilities to innovate and communicate. Less corporate, but just as important in promoting design and designers in the last decade, have been independent retailers and manufacturers like Thorsten van Elten, writers such as Max Fraser, public relations firms such as Camron, design magazines like *Icon* and gallerists such as Libby Sellers, The Carpenters Workshop Gallery and Gallery Fumi.

Can we learn anything about British attitudes towards design by looking at design policy elsewhere? It may help to consider two extremes: the Netherlands and the United States. In the Netherlands design is centrally subsidized and nationally and internationally promoted, giving designers status and security, and their works cultural significance. In the United States, design depends almost entirely on the private sector. As a result in the Netherlands public spaces and services are overtly, consciously designed, sending out a message that design is embedded culturally, socially and politically, whereas in the United States the opposite is true. There, conspicuously designed public services and spaces are mainly seen to indicate profligate waste of public money within the political context of a right-wing press that agitates for less government spending.[27] Britain lies somewhere in between the two. On rare occasions public money enables great examples of civic design, for example recent stations on London Underground's Jubilee Line, opened in 1999, or social initiatives like the Design Council's 'Joined up Design for Schools' scheme. But too much top-heavy governmental intervention produces incoherent results like the Dome and policies that help no one. Private enterprise and the market seldom achieve truly inspiring designs, just branded landscapes, like the Bluewater (1999) or Westfield (2008, 2011) shopping centres. In Britain it seems we prefer the middle way, neither totally free-market nor centrally controlled.

This is the context within which designers work here. Britain today can give them great opportunities (through networks, patronage and education, for example) but also frustrating constraints (for instance the lack of structured institutional or commercial support, and the expense of living and working). What further connections can we make between the diverse designers in this book? One strong theme is an interest in time-based media and performance.

Sixty years ago Charles and Ray Eames made films and presentations as well as designing furniture. They ignored conventional boundaries between disciplines and embraced the notion of performance as a means of communicating their design ideas. In different ways their influence persists, and perhaps the extent to which the notion of performance recurs throughout work in this book can be traced to the Eameses. We see it in the theatricality of installations by designers as diverse as Troika and Jaime Hayon, where impressive and immersive experiences are created to promote the brand values of corporate clients. We see it in the prevailing trend for digital interactivity in the works of rAndom International, Moritz Waldemeyer and Simon Heijdens who all make works that move and respond to time and place. Noam Toran and Onkar Kular immerse themselves in cinematic cultural references. At its most extreme Glithero, Martino Gamper, Julia Lohmann and Max Lamb perform their acts of designing and making: the performances themselves are a vital element of their practices. A performance requires a subject and viewer, and our gaze is held by increasingly audacious (often sophisticated and subtle, and occasionally pretentious) technical and aesthetic statements by all these designers. By appealing to more senses and incorporating time and action as well as materials and structure, performance-based design interprets and directly communicates a designer's intentions in a way that a static object alone simply cannot.

Terms such as 'hybridity' and 'interdisciplinarity' are frequently used to discuss new or peculiar turns in culture, including design culture, but we have difficulty in defining them. In the context of design practice, what do we mean? Are we referring to designers with broad repertoires of skills, allowing them to move between disciplines with ease like Glithero, who make objects and films? Or perhaps we mean highly specialized technicians, like Moritz Waldemeyer, who cross an invisible creative line to become designers or artists in their own right. Are we really talking about the blurring of conventional boundaries between 'old-fashioned' definitions of practice? 'I think the labels "artist" and "designer" are outdated, they don't have relevance anymore',[28] says Simon Heijdens, but I am not sure I entirely agree. Even if they are outdated, they still provide context and discourses, helping us to understand and interpret work that, in many ways, is new and therefore inclined to be alien and inaccessible. In a shifting world old certainties can provide structure even when they are being challenged. Martino Gamper explains what the differences mean to him: 'I'm a designer in that my work is functional and I care about the usability of my products but an artist in that I like to think about what my work means in its particular context. And I create like a craftsman, using traditional tools to make things out of other things.'[29]

If the range of design practice in this book could be represented along a line, with mass-produced industrial products at one extreme and art installations at the other, we might find Industrial Facility at a far remove from Onkar Kular and Noam Toran. But strangely enough, in very different ways, Sam Hecht and Kular and Toran place the neutralized, decoded industrial artefact at the heart of their practices, and instead of a linear chart we should be thinking of a Venn diagram with 'the thing', or 'the product' at its centre, upon which all these designers variously reflect.

Small wonder, then, that these people sometimes baulk at describing themselves as 'only' designers. Hannes Koch describes the members of his studio, rAndom International, as 'media artists', while Jaime Hayon prefers to call himself a 'creator', rather than limit himself as a designer or an artist. They and others move happily between digital design, craft, mass production and one-off artworks. Some of these practitioners, such as Noam Toran and Onkar Kular, and Committee make work that is about design but looks more like fine art, or is informed by a critical perspective outside industrial design. Patrik Fredrikson and Ian Stallard feel the same: 'We have a constant love affair with the freedom of the fine art world, but as we always tend to pull this inspiration into functional objects, we must, at the end of the day, call ourselves designers.'[30] Those designers who are immersed in designing for industry, like Industrial Facility and Klauser and Carpenter, are also aware of the communicative and cultural value of designed objects and the role they play in society. Other designers are less focused on designing products for the market. William Wiles has observed, 'Designers like rAndom International and Troika are a challenge to linear, engineer-driven technological progress. They pose instead a romantic, chaotic and non-linear approach, based on designing with no end product in mind – a "Victorian approach" of tinkering and experimenting.'[31]

A characteristic of new graduates is their determination to go it alone as independent designers as soon as they can. In the past more designers would join established studios immediately after leaving education, to find their feet and gain professional experience. The odds are stacked against a lone practitioner who lacks resources, access to specialisms and expertise, and possibly even a studio of their own. One innovative model is to form a loose collective of like-minded souls who can (in the words of one writer) 'share bills and honest feedback'.[32] A well-known design collective is OKAY Studio, formed in 2006 in Stoke Newington, north London. Peter Marigold and Raw Edges of OKAY are profiled separately elsewhere in this book, but the group also includes Tomás Alonso, Oscar Narud and others. Together the collective encapsulates a prevailing character of British design, defined by the *Art Newspaper* as 'a common thread of funkiness, an improvised or provisional quality that runs through all their work'.[33] Their former RCA tutor, Daniel Charny, considered the collective to be built upon a federative model where 'the group … share a studio, a workshop, a very small kitchen, tools and bicycle pumps, nicknames and jargon, healthy competition, unreserved rallying to each other's success, proclaimed envies and the odd night out.'[34]

'We don't work together', says Shay Alkalay of Raw Edges, explaining the dynamics of a design collective. 'We all do different types of design. But we share a space and we're great friends, like a family.' The difference between this and most families is that this one has members from Israel, the Netherlands, Japan, Spain, Germany, Norway and Britain. This melting pot of nationalities met at the RCA, and the diversity typifies not only the college but multicultural Britain too. 'If you go to Milan, you realize that most of the people are Italian and you are a foreigner', says Alkalay. 'If you come to Britain, you're like – where are all the English people?'[35] They are Deyan Sudjic's 'British by choice rather than birth' designers. This is not to say they have ceded their own nationalities or gained British passports (none of them have), but that they elected to stay and work here. It remains to be seen whether proposed changes to immigration law that curtails the time graduates can remain after they have studied in the UK, will be the legislation that kills off this kind of multinational collective.

In conclusion, can we say what makes design in Britain so vital, diverse and innovative? To a large degree I think it is due to the conditions that Mark Leonard described in *Britain™* almost 15 years ago. Britain is known as an international hub for creativity, innovation and knowledge, whose cultural and educational institutions respect and appeal to the best minds from overseas as well as from the UK. Our heritage as a colonial power has been overlaid and superseded by a strong sense of fair play, tolerance, multiculturalism and internationalism, moderated by mainly liberal democratic politics. In Britain we are open to the new and innovative because we respect and retain the context of the old and conservative. We conform to non-conformism and delight in being the outsiders. These are just the right conditions for freethinking designers to thrive.

El Ultimo Grito

'Let's claim a place for the "designer-eccentrics".'

Spanish designers Roberto Feo (born 1964) and Rosario Hurtado (born 1966) grew up in Madrid and studied in London before founding their partnership in 1997. Despite a brief period in Berlin they have been based in London ever since, and are the longest established studio in this book. They work on furniture, graphics and interior projects, and between commercial and critical design. Some El Ultimo Grito designs have entered production, including lighting with Mathmos and multipurpose children's furniture for Magis. But the designers are equally well known for their installations and exhibitions, for example at the Stanley Picker Gallery at Kingston University or in galleries in Barcelona, Berlin and Madrid. For these events they often use unconventional materials, like stickers, to create sculptural furniture objects (fig.6). Feo and Hurtado self-publish manifestos and collections of writing, and curate exhibitions of their own work and that of their peers and students at Shopwork, their gallery and studio space in south-east London, and most notably in the show *Nowhere/Now/Here* at LABoral, a centre for art and industrial design in Gijón, northern Spain (2008).

Outspoken and non-conformist, throughout their projects they question the possibilities and roles of design. Feo and Hurtado teach in London at the Royal College of Art and Goldsmith's College as well as elsewhere across Europe, and primarily because of their pedagogy they have been very influential on the subsequent generation of designers.

Gareth Williams: You have said, 'We try to make a point of questioning the status quo, but we don't regard ourselves as radicals'.[1] Elsewhere you have commented, 'People say we're alternative, but I think we're mainstream', but also, 'Subversive is the only thing you can aspire to be as a designer. If everyone were complacent, everything would remain the same. If you have a problem, you try to find a solution. Design is a survival instinct.'[2]

I'm confused. On the one hand you seem to be deliberately making yourselves outsiders, to look inside. On the other you claim to be as ordinary as the rest of us. There is a tension here that I would like you to explore. It is almost as if you are making yourselves uncomfortable outsiders as a mechanism to reveal the 'truth' about mainstream culture. Can you elaborate?

El Ultimo Grito: To be an outsider is not about being outside the system but about being able to look at the system from as near to the outside as you can. The outsiders are able to assess the system in a new light because they do not share (or choose to ignore) the specific set of cultural rules that apply to the specific situation. Our interest lies on these edges, which we try to explore, and invite others to come and enjoy the views from here. In that sense the ambition of our work is always mainstream. But mainstream should not be mistaken here with consumerism. The mainstream is about shared cultural values, which in any progressive society will be in a

constant state of flux thanks to the activities of people who question these values.

Gareth Williams: 'There is a new interest in trying to explore ideas in a different way that is not linked to an idea of what the market wants', you have said. 'There's more interest in going back to the vision of a designer and trying to propose new things for consumers.'[3] You are part of a wave of designers who act absolutely autonomously but who sometimes only really seem to value dialogue with other designers. It can seem that you are quite designer-centric. Are you aware of this in yourselves?

El Ultimo Grito: It was an important breakthrough for us to understand that we were using our work to explain design to ourselves. The work helped us understand what we were doing, and necessarily the thoughts that sprawl from these activities had to become part of our construct of design. This is the reason why our work takes so many different avenues and we would still call it design. From this point of view, you could say that our work is designer-centric although we understand it more as a design-centred dialogue.

We believe that the language of our work is one of encouragement to reclaim our design instinct as humans, to apply it to our lives both as creators and users. Its ultimate aim is to generate a direct dialogue with the rest of the world, beyond the design arena, where alternatives to the design of design can be truly discussed without the interference of the 'discipline'. We have always intended that our work should demystify design and make it more transparent and accessible, allowing you to engage with it and understand the thinking process and the rationale of how it is produced, and empowering you to apply this knowledge into new ideas about design. We advocate the designer as a post-disciplinary figure, a kind of 'apprentice of everything and master of nothing', an active participant in the construction of our shared image of ourselves,

the world, the universe… Let's claim a place for the 'designer-eccentrics'.

Gareth Williams: Is it really possible to be commercially experimental? You have said, 'We have always worked between the experimental and the commercial, the two running parallel and feeding from each other. This self-feeding process has always been part of our work and we think it has enriched it.'[4] Aren't these mutually exclusive positions?

El Ultimo Grito: Design history is populated with examples of successful commercially experimental design. Industry and society have always been prepared to accept and embrace changes brought upon by technological means. Technological experimentation, in short, materializes in three different ways: first through new products, which a new technology makes possible; secondly through new methods of production; and thirdly through new materials. Producers and consumers are ready to assimilate these kinds of changes as long as they are commercially viable both in terms of production and consumption.

The products of experimental design that question the cultural aspects of society are much more difficult to implement, firstly because it would take a massive effort to communicate them, but mainly because they propose alternatives to the cultural construct, and this is very hard to accept at a small and grand scale. To change cultural habits requires a big effort in terms of communication and education. This is why it is mostly only achieved either as a by-product or by force (through laws, regulations, etc.). Still, this is the area of design that interests us the most and where we develop our work.

In our practice, we do not separate the experimental or the commercial. Our most experimental projects started as commercial work. We use commissioned projects, and the

resources they provide, to generate opportunities to test new ideas in the public arena. This is how we started our work with stickers, producing pop-up shops and temporary spaces for Griffin, the fashion label (2003). Afterwards we pushed this project further, using it to explore new typologies and as a way of liberating our process from the dictatorship of certain materials, and at the same time questioning that an acceptable product finish is one defined by industry (figs 7 and 8).

Another example would be the 'Mico' objects for Magis (2006, fig. 9). Initially Magis approached us to produce a collection of children's clothing, but when we presented the clothes we also showed them the 'Mico' designs. Our objective was not to create something that would introduce the child into our grown-up culture, but to open up other ways to relate to objects. The objects were designed so that every position would contain a different character, abstract and figurative at the same time. They are not specifically furniture but contain 'functional accidents' and are the right dimensions for children to explore them in a physical way. Eugenio Perazza, the owner of Magis, loved the 'Mico' from the beginning, but there were many internal discussions about their viability and how to communicate products with no precedent or obvious typology. Finally it was decided that the only way to deal with this new typology was to call it *Oggetto Polivalente* meaning, in Italian, multipurpose object.

Ultimately, it all depends on what is considered commercial. We consider an installation in a public space, a publication and a product for the furniture industry as both commercial and research work, and every time we try to experiment. To be experimental is more a question of how far can you go with your ideas in every specific context, how far can you push your design language so it can still be understood.

6. (*page 31, previously*)
100m bench, 2007
La Casa Encendida, Madrid

7. (*opposite*)
Peckham Shield table, 2010
Design Products Collection,
Royal College of Art

8. (*left*)
Tape chair, 2006

9. (*below, left and right*)
Mico object prototypes, 2006

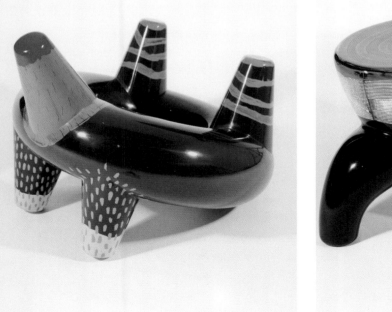

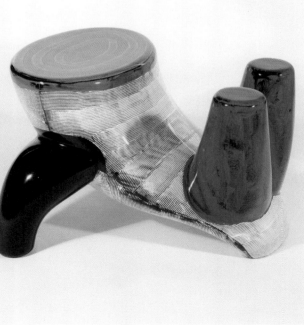

2

Raw Edges

'You get more work done by dividing it in two: you have two brains, two pairs of hands.'

Every design couple is defined by the internal dynamics of their professional and personal lives, and Yael Mer and Shay Alkalay are no different. In many respects their life experience is identical. They were both born in 1976 in Tel Aviv, and both studied first at the Bezalel Academy in Jerusalem and then under Ron Arad at the Royal College of Art, graduating in 2006, the year they also married. As part of OKAY Studio, a design collective of RCA graduates, they share the same friends, influences, exhibitions and London studio space. Mer and Alkalay even shared work experience in China but only in 2007 did they formalize their professional partnership, founding their studio Raw Edges.

Why 'Raw Edges'? Aside from sounding like the name of a 1980s rock band (which they relish), they chose the peculiar name because they like designs that are not 'over-cooked', that in production still retain the spontaneity of a prototype or design concept, and because of their fondness for materials whose edges can be left rough and unfinished, like leather, paper or felt. That list of materials reveals another characteristic, this time more associated with one designer than the other. Mer found an interest in folding and creasing two-dimensional materials into three-dimensional forms. A good early example is the series of milk cartons she made for her RCA graduation project, which swell progressively plumper to indicate the level of fat in their contents. Alkalay, on the other hand, likes to explore the potential of motion and reaction in a design. While she has a strong interest in pattern-cutting, tailoring and fashion, he likes to put things together that move, for example 'Pivot' (2008), an innovative set of drawers that are hinged rather than slide, now manufactured by Dutch firm Arco. It may sound like Alkalay's and Mer's concerns are predictably gendered, but these differences of interest lie at the heart of their practice, giving it diversity and depth. 'You get more work done by dividing it in two: you have two brains, two pairs of hands', says Mer.[1]

An intimate partnership does not mean they cannot work independently, and Raw Edge's strength lies in the two designers' guidance and criticism of each other's work. 'I really like movement', says Alkalay. 'I spent most of my childhood playing with toys where you have to build or make stuff – it was all to do with connections.' Mer steered his interest towards designing a chest of drawers because 'it's the only furniture that moves'.[2] In 2007 Alkalay developed an extraordinary chest of drawers that appeared to be frameless. In fact, the frame is concealed inside allowing the drawers to extend both forwards and backwards. Descriptively called 'Stack' (fig.10), the tapered overlapping drawers look like weatherboarding. Alkalay built an enormous stack of drawers, 4.5 metres high, in the hall of a South Kensington mansion that Martino Gamper had occupied for *Gradual*, an exhibition of recent RCA graduates during the London Design Festival. The Johnson Trading Gallery subsequently took this version to New York but Mark Holmes, at the time the design director of Established & Sons, saw a smaller version shown elsewhere during the same festival. He launched it as the centrepiece of the firm's Milan furniture fair exhibition in April 2008, and 'Stack' went on to gain critical acclaim, before receiving the accolade of acquisition by the Museum of Modern Art in New York. Such swift ascent of international design's slippery pole is rare, but success did not adversely affect the mild-mannered designer. It did, however, focus attention on Raw Edges' other projects.

In 2009, still only fairly recently out of college, Raw Edges was named Designer of the Future at Design Miami/Basel (along with Tomáš Gabzdil Libertíny, Nacho Carbonell and fellow OKAY Studio colleague Peter Marigold). For the exhibition Mer and Alkalay built 'Mount Domesticus', a plasterboard mountainscape reflected in a 'lake' of heavily polished stained oak parquet. The floor was later developed for an exhibition at Established & Sons' London gallery during the Frieze Art Fair in 2009 (fig.11), from where it was installed in Stella McCartney's Milan store.

Also in 2009 the studio was invited to take part in *Craft Punk*, an exhibition organized by Design Miami/Basel director Ambra Medda for the luxury brand Fendi during the Milan furniture fair. For this project they declined to use the company's signature material, leather, but focused instead on their folding techniques, creating 'Pleated Pleat' (figs 14 and 15), a domed paper form into which they injected foam. In a sense this was the opposite of upholstery, where a cover is stretched over a pre-formed mass. Here, the shape of the cover dictated the final form of the furniture in a process more akin to designing clothing, where it is easy to change the shape of a garment by adjusting the pattern.

The designers developed their idea into a series of 'Tailored Wood' stools (2008, figs 12 and 13) that look a little like brown paper bags twisted closed. In fact, they were made by pouring liquid foam into a wood veneer shell. As the foam expanded and set, it caused each stool to crinkle in individual ways and Mer likens the process of making them by hand to performance. The first edition was made for FAT Gallery in Paris, from which Italian furniture supremo Giulio Cappellini developed them for industrial production. 'It's what you call a post-industrial product', he said. 'It is produced in an industrial way, but each piece is unique.' Mer explained their thinking: 'I enjoy working with material and not forcing something on it, but seeing what the tendency is for the material, and it was amazing that Cappellini wanted to keep this randomness … I was doing all these sketches of chairs and sofas and then making patterns on my computer, which I would print out on A4 paper and fold to create tiny, sweet mock-ups, and I really wanted to keep that sketchy feel.'[3] The 'Tailored Wood' stools have led to a family of chairs and sofas called 'Volume'.

12. (*right*)
Tailored Wood stool, 2010
Manufactured by Cappellini, Italy

13. (*below*)
Tailored Wood stool, production
process, 2008

The designers have developed the notion of a material as both upholstery and structure with the 'Coiling Collection' (2010). The coils are distorted in the way it is possible to push the centre of a tailor's tape measure into a cone, a principle previously exploited by Georg Baldele for his 'Caveman' lights (1998). Raw Edges have made furniture and rugs from strips of felt that are made rigid by applying Jesmonite, a type of resin. 'We like the contrast', explains Mer. 'The appearance of the felt as a simple, warm, soft, natural and old material and on the other hand the silicon, which is more technical, futuristic, glossy, sophisticated material.'[4] The results are comic, somewhat awkward and characterful, and reminiscent of furniture by El Ultimo Grito; Roberto Feo was their tutor and both designers gained experience in his studio during their student years.

Raw Edges have enjoyed remarkable success in a very brief period. Their challenge is to maintain the connection of their hands-on studio practice to ever more ambitious industrial projects. For now they remain very grounded. 'Our work is very intuitive, but we don't create abstract things that can't be manufactured or don't have a practical function', says Alkalay. 'We should remember that our work still needs to be connected to society. If people don't understand what we're doing or don't want to use it, if it's just a personal expression of our own ideas, then it doesn't really work as good design.'[5]

14.
Pleated Pleat stool,
production process, 2009

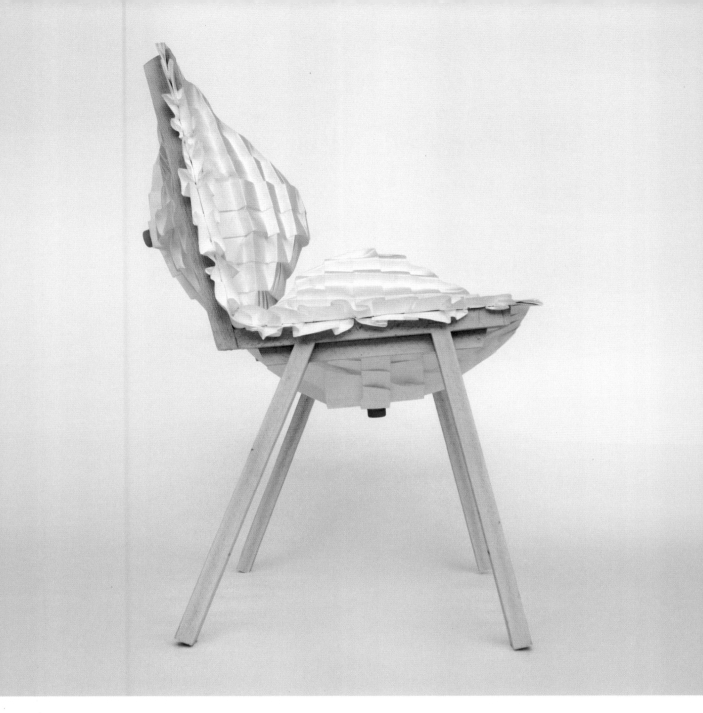

15.
Pleated Pleat chair, 2009

3

Peter Marigold

'All of my works are based on a kind of "investigation by destruction"... I'm motivated by dissatisfaction with the way things are.'

Peter Marigold's work is all about the clash of opposites. Or we can say it is about the complement of extremes. Whichever way you look at it, his work (mostly furniture) represents a tension between two poles or viewpoints. Two such extremes are making and breaking, and Marigold says 'All of my works are based on a kind of "investigation by destruction" … I'm motivated by dissatisfaction with the way things are.'[1]

Marigold (born 1974), trained as a sculptor and worked as a stage designer before enrolling at the Royal College of Art to study Design Products under Ron Arad in 2004, an experience he repeatedly says was life changing. The art world's self-consciousness dissatisfied him, whereas design and craft appeared to offer honesty and simplicity (a view shared by fellow artist-trained designers, Committee). Although the substantial, furniture-sized scale of some work is often attributed to his sculptural background, Marigold claims it was the imperatives of designing high-visibility theatre sets and props that informed this. Critics have regarded him as a latter-day craftsman because of the honest, woody and handmade character of his furniture, though I think this is his artistic training revealing itself in his conceptual thinking. In any case, his use of timber is circumstantial, and he claims to have no strong affinity with it, despite its loaded cultural status as a furniture material. It is simply that it is readily available and quick to use, and Marigold admits to lacking patience. Once pieces are finished 'I can't wait to get rid of them, and get them out of the door', he says. 'I'm really not interested in highly finished products.'[2]

David McFadden, Chief Curator of New York's Museum of Arts and Design has observed: 'Marigold's work is an example of the juxtaposition of the extremely refined with the extremely crude. It's the design version of the raw and cooked.'[3] Tensions and opposites abound in Marigold's work: between the inside and outside of objects, solid and void, refined and raw materials, ancient and modern, chaos and order, destruction and construction. A breakthrough in Marigold's design came when he realized that splitting a log into angled pieces and then inverting them still resulted in a 360-degree form. By turning the form inside out he made it into something entirely new. The first expression of this was a series of oblique shelves called 'Split' (2007, in the background of the photograph on page 43), reminiscent of stacked fruit crates, each featuring split logs as horizontal corner blocks. Marigold later refined the idea for commercial production by SCP, renaming it 'SUM'. Turned vertically, and split along the length of entire tree boughs, the blocks became the supports for a series of seven serpentine shelf units called 'Octave' made for Gallery Libby Sellers (2007). 'There is the discovery of forms within forms, and fundamental underlying logics in nature are something that can also be seen in musical instruments', Marigold has stated, explaining why each shelf included a sound hole decorated with marquetry like a guitar.[4] The following year Marigold designed the 'Thin Slice' cabinet and 'Yield' screen for Libby Sellers, which she included in her pop-up exhibition, *Beau Sauvage*, at Liberty in London, alongside work by Max Lamb and others. For these Marigold continued to explore wood in an almost natural state, this time splitting eucalyptus logs to create thin slats to clad the furniture, showing the wood's internal structure in order, in Seller's words, 'to bring the unseen inside out'.[5]

Marigold's 'Palindrome' series of furniture continued to play with the tension between the inside and outside of an object, and was first shown at Design Miami/Basel in 2009 (fig.16), where he was one of the nominated Designers of the Future. Here, one side is made by casting acrylic, reinforced with fibreglass, in a wooden mould. The opposite side is the mould itself, dismantled and turned inside out. The whole becomes like a curious reflection of itself which, like a palindrome, is the same read from either end, a new and curious way of adapting symmetry in design. Although Marigold makes the various one-off 'Palindrome' pieces himself, for sale through Moss in New York and with Phillips de Pury in London, his original sketch for a wardrobe miraculously doubled in size by a mirror which inspired the entire series, is now in production with the young Italian brand Skitsch.

The 'Dug and Stuff' vessels (2010, fig.17) explore the relationship between inside and outside, solid and void, presence and absence, and destruction and construction.[6] These works are nominally vessels (in that

they each contain space) and are made by casting in clay the voids carved within timber logs. Marigold fills the void entirely with clay before hollowing its centre with his thumbs. This action displaces the clay, ejecting an extrusion from the mould's mouth bearing the surface marks of the timber. At this point, Marigold opens the split mould to remove the vessel and takes the opportunity to expand the void by carving out more timber. He may repeat this up to 12 times, to create a series of vessels from small to large, made in a single expanding mould. The split wooden mould, still bearing the shape of a tree trunk, is often displayed with the vessels, and each vessel is mounted on a wire stand, like some ancient amphora. The archaeological character is intentional. He has written of the project: 'Creativity, for me, has always been a process of both destruction and reconstruction – sometimes more like archaeology than design.'[7] The crude clay vessels record the roughly carved timber void at each stage, and the processes of destruction and preservation determine one another.

There are comparisons with Rachel Whiteread's sculptures, but neither lay claim to inventing casting. However they take different approaches. With 'Dug and Stuff' Marigold casts and re-carves the same mould, gradually expanding the interior void until, inevitably, the mould fails. 'Palindrome' includes the mould and the cast equally together, questioning the authenticity or primacy of both components. Marigold's vessels would be more accurate representations of the inside of the wooden mould if he used silicon or lost-wax processes, so his crude use of clay is intentional, as is the rough and approximate quality of the carving itself. Beauty, evidently, is not the project's aim (there is no attempt to match the refined quality of Whiteread's casts). Rather, our accepted notions of beauty would interfere with the uncompromised rawness of these cast and carved voids, and their archaeological overtones. Their primitiveness and immediacy are their essential qualities and are what, for me, elevate all Marigold's best work.

It is Marigold's willingness to expose his ideas and processes so candidly, without finish or justification, even when they are, to be frank, less than beautiful or useful, which makes him a significant design voice. Lacking the branded slickness of too many product designers, he is the artistic outsider who can shake up design's conventions. 'I think creating banal objects that are highly polished but have no substance is a bit of a crime', he concludes.[8]

4

Max Lamb

'My work is not about keeping secrets ... I want people to see every detail of how it was made, and understand the material.'

In terms of Max Lamb's design and techniques, his work is relatively straightforward and accessible, which in part probably accounts for the considerable attention and success he has enjoyed in the five or so years since he graduated from the Royal College of Art. Many of his works (he prefers to call them 'projects') are monumental chairs in one form or another, and he has worked in steel, granite, copper, bronze, pewter and plaster. Perhaps it is the easy comparison to minimalist artists such as Scott Burton (though he does not share their aesthetic agenda) that has made him attractive to high-end collectors. His furniture is sometimes challenging but never frightening, tasteless or offensive. It is strong, and rather polite.

There have been many accolades since Lamb graduated in 2006. Tom Dixon immediately hired him, but he left a year later to set up his own studio. In just a few years he has enjoyed several international residencies, won a Designer of the Future award at the Design Miami/ Basel fair in 2008, completed commissions for major patrons and joined a New York gallery. The key to understanding his success is that he does not overcomplicate things with layers of design philosophy, but sets out to make quite rudimentary furniture forms that clearly communicate their materials and the techniques he has used. 'I try to be true to a material, generally using the material alone and in its elemental form', he says. 'I want to celebrate and exploit each material for its inherent visual and functional characteristics, properties and qualities ... I never try to force a material, but rather steer it into a form that is functional yet appears to have happened spontaneously, as if by nature.'[1] This talk about harmony with nature might give the impression that Lamb designs intuitively, but that is not the case. 'Sometimes the object is "made" rather than "designed", meaning the design is a consequence of the

process which in turn is a consequence of the material', he explains.[2] I think Lamb intently seeks maximum results from minimum intervention, and he chooses his intervention carefully depending on the character of the material to hand (fig.19). This is not a radical position for a designer or an artist, but it is effective.

As well as liking to explore materials, Lamb has a passion for 'do-it-yourself' self-sufficiency that springs from a belief that making your own objects gives them value and longevity. He wants his designs to enable others to make their own furniture, so he has designed chairs for self-assembly. One, simply called the 'DIY' chair, can be put together from 31 identical lengths of timber; he published instructions on how to make it in *Apartamento* magazine. Another, designed for the Japanese manufacturer E&Y in 2010, is called 'Third', because the designer, the manufacturer and the consumer each need to do a third of the work. Both chairs successfully and economically address mass seating: why, then, does Lamb not design more for industry?

The 'do-it-yourself' instinct extends to his own production methods too. Lamb wanted to cast a stool from metal but, frustrated at his inability to access industrial scale facilities in a foundry, he created his own foundry on a Cornish beach near where he grew up (he was born in St Austell in 1980). The result was 'Pewter' stool (2006). 'I bore the holes and carve the shape into the sand, heat the ingots of pewter in my mum's old saucepan on a camping stove then pour it directly in the shape', he explains. 'I like the way I can go to the beach and leave with a finished product without doing any secondary work like filing the metal down; the purity is appealing.'[3] The rising water table can affect the length of the legs, so he designed it with three legs that would always make contact with the ground, even if they were uneven. As with many designers in this book, he filmed the process of making the stools, and later desks (figs 20 and 21), and the film is as much the end product as the objects themselves, both contributing to our understanding of his processes to achieve the final work. The legs of the stool are granular and retain the impression of the sand, while the seat surface is smooth where the pewter was exposed to the sea air. He has commented, 'My work is not about keeping secrets … I want people to see every detail of how it was made, and understand the material'.[4] This project, which made his early reputation, is not so much a reinvention of craft as an explanation of industrial production. Like many of the designers in this book, Lamb is reclaiming techniques that are alien to most of us, with the ambition of empowering us all.

Lamb's biggest production has been a series of carved stone furniture made in situ in quarries (fig.18). Generally he makes just two cuts into

Max Lamb

20. (*opposite*)
Pewter desk, production
process on Caerhays beach,
Cornwall, 2011

a raw boulder to create the seat and back, which are then polished. The first series was hewn from Cornish granite, but the next collection took him to An Li Stone, a quarry at Chengnanzhuang, Hebei Province, 350km south-west of Beijing, where he spent a two-week residency organized by Chinese International Gallery Exposition in conjunction with Vitra Design Museum. The 15 pieces that resulted were shown during the London Design Festival in 2009. A third collection, shown by the Johnson Trading Gallery in New York, was made from Delaware Bluestone from the Catskill Mountains, the characteristic stone of New York City sidewalks. These massive, barely useable items of furniture do not further debates about design, or its relation to art, but are easy for the art market to appreciate during a period when the work of young designers has been much hyped. Terms such as 'site-specific' and 'locally global production' might be used to elevate the projects (though Lamb does not use them). In fact, using local stone in different locations to make variant yet characteristic and consistent forms is a clever adaptation of the art world's production of limited editions. So it would probably be wrong to find some kind of statement about Cornish or British identity in Lamb's use of beaches or quarries, as these are merely expedient local resources that he willingly substitutes when he can, rather than symbolic gestures about nationhood.

More interesting, from a technical though perhaps not an aesthetic point of view, has been the 'Poly' furniture (2006, fig.19). Lamb's starting point was expanded polystyrene that he carved roughly with a claw hammer to create chair shapes. The carving is swift and must be satisfying to do, but the material is not durable or fit for purpose as furniture. He solved this in two ways, firstly by coating the polystyrene forms with heavy-duty rubber to protect and preserve them. These chairs can be compared to Fredrikson Stallard's 'Pyrenees' sofa, in that both are formed by hand from lightweight industrial materials that are then coated for durability, adding value and functionality. Lamb extended the idea by carving and coating large blocks of polystyrene that he called 'Shelters', so large they contained caves big enough to enter. The Johnson Trading Gallery showed these in Miami. The second intervention with the polystyrene was more radical, and returned Lamb to sand casting. Here, he buried the chairs in sand and when he poured in molten bronze the polystyrene evaporated leaving a solid metal cast of the fragile original (2008). This is a new iteration of the ancient lost-wax technique.

The brief for those feted as 'designers of the future' by the Design Miami/Basel fair in 2008 was unusual: they were invited to work with concrete and wool. Lamb, who shared the award with Julia Lohmann, Martino Gamper and Kram/Weisshaar, was the most experimental of the group, creating a series of stools called 'Solids of Revolution'. Formally akin to the Eames's famous 'Time Life' turned-wood stool, Lamb's furniture used two materials with surprisingly similar qualities. One set was turned from very high-density wool felt, usually manufactured to make polishing pads for industrial applications like stone finishing. The remaining stools were lathe-turned from low density autoclaved cellular concrete, a foamed material containing a high volume of air in a cell-like structure, five times lighter than conventional concrete, highly insulating, and easy to machine. The two completely opposing materials turned out to be similar in weight and character. It seems a pity that the project ended with these collectible items, when the materials would appear to have great potential for mass-produced furniture.

In 2010 Lamb was commissioned to make a one-off piece for the headquarters of HSBC Private Bank. It is the kind of special project that suits his talents and temperament. The texture of his work, entitled 'The Vermiculated Ashlar', was cast from the rusticated podium of the 1840s building designed by Sydney Smirke, housing the bank in London's St James's. With this cast he made a block of hard plaster with the character of sandstone, which he carved by hand to form a bench on a rusticated plinth. Before it was installed in the bank, it was shown alongside plaster casts of famous sculptures in the Cast Courts at the V&A, reinforcing the temptation to think of this work as a contemporary sculpture rather than a seat. Lamb even talks about his work in a sculptor's terms, preferring to leave the signs of his chisel on the material as evidence of his hand at work. Speaking not of this project, but about his work in general terms, Lamb concludes 'I accept that the outcome is often "crude" but I guess this describes my methods of making. My work is like the signature at the end of a typed letter – the only part which is scribed by hand – the part with character and imperfection. The deft hand is capable of producing and reproducing seemingly perfect forms, details and decorations, but in the machine age perfection has become so easy and banal. The hardest thing to ask of a machine is to create what the hand does effortlessly.'[5]

5

Simon Hasan

'I don't see myself as a craftsman. I'm a product designer, and I would never be so arrogant as to call myself a craftsman. It takes people a lifetime to master these skills.'

Craft techniques and, more significantly, their symbolic and political relevance inform all Simon Hasan's work. 'I don't see myself as a craftsman', he has said. 'I'm a product designer, and I would never be so arrogant as to call myself a craftsman. It takes people a lifetime to master these skills.'[1] It is impossible not to consider his boiled leather or 'Cleft Oak' (fig.24) works outside perennial debates about the relationship between craft and industry, hand and machine, or the virtuous craftsman and the oppressed worker. This is because most of his output derives from a traditional but neglected technique of hardening leather called *cuir bouilli*. Known since the Middle Ages, the process involves soaking tanned leather to make it pliable before briefly boiling it, at which point the tannins are melted, allowing the leather to be reformed on a mould. Once dry it is hard and brittle, both strong and capable of taking intricate decoration. *Cuir bouilli* leather was suitable for armour, and was used to make flasks, boxes and for bookbinding. As with so many medieval crafts, it enjoyed a revival in the late nineteenth century. Now as then, *cuir bouilli* is a technique that resonates with real and imagined notions of arcane guilds, ancient and lost skills, and benign but feudal social systems.

Simon Hasan (born 1973) does not make armour, or bind books. Instead he uses the technique, which he discovered while at the Royal College of Art, to make vases and even furniture. His work is not a direct and wholesale revival of a craft tradition but an adaptation of it to present conditions. Therefore he is able to say he is not a craftsman,

but a designer who uses knowledge of craft to make objects that are commentaries on both the state of craft and its position in relation to industrial production. If his principle interest is actually industry, not craft (he envisages a 'boutique factory system' where craftsmanship and industrial production are united) one could say his crafted work is actually *about* industrial production. This is a deft piece of doublethink that simultaneously promises direct engagement with a subject while also retaining distance from it. More generously, it could be said that designers like Hasan are discovering personal destinations for their work in the well-trodden pathways of craft and design.

Hasan is aware of the complex ambiguities that his work represents and he explores them. Northampton is the traditional home of British leather craft and for the Northampton Festival in 2010 Hasan delivered 'Industrial Makeshifts' (fig.22), a vending machine to sell his *cuir bouilli* vessels: a provocative act in which medieval heritage collided with modern retailing. 'A vending machine is probably the most impersonal way of purchasing something I can think of', he said. 'It's the automated end-point of global industry – an extreme form of distribution even for a conventional, mass-produced object. I like the contrasts and contradictions it throws up.'[2] Elaborating his point, he has commented elsewhere, 'The vending machine is a useful icon, a visual shorthand for talking about issues such as globalized industry, mass production, cost and value – all the things we don't expect in a hand-crafted object. I love this contradiction, and as a designer I'm interested in looking at how I might be able to reconcile these two opposing worlds.'[3]

Since they seemingly exist primarily as discursive illustrations of his design ethos, does it matter whether Hasan's *cuir bouilli* works are well designed? It took him a year at the RCA to perfect his technique but the first vases were formed around crude wooden moulds and bore the marks of their fabrication (fig.23). He sealed them with resin that also added a splash of colour. 'The moulds have an accidental quality that's hard to design, but the spray paint adds a necessary sense of delicacy', he has said.[4] Over time the vessels have gained more refinement. Shown with the vases at his 2008 degree show was a stool entirely made of leather, with no other structure. Regardless of whether they met basic functional requirements the works conformed to a necessary pre-condition for craft and design today, which is that they were in a signature style that Hasan has made his own. Moreover, each variant is individual and the production methods lend themselves to serial, numbered production. They are collectible. These works were never intended for the mass market and Hasan sees himself as a gallery-oriented designer. This self-awareness, and ability to position his work in broader commercial contexts, perhaps arises from his previous career in

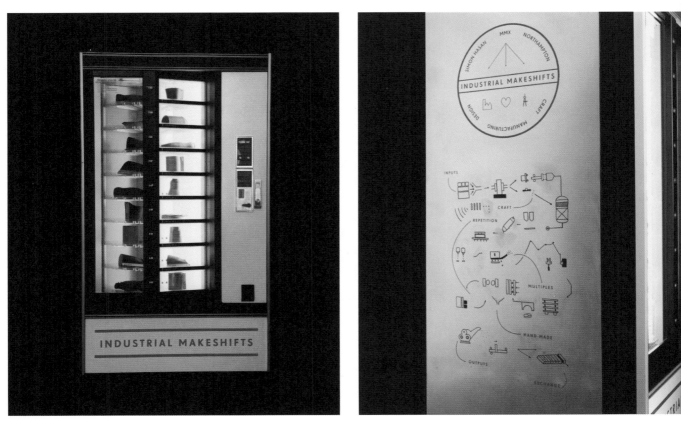

advertising and a first degree in marketing. 'I don't want to live like an artist for the rest of my life … [I] need to create value beyond the next commission to create a viable career and business.'[5]

In 2008 a scholarship enabled Hasan to tour Britain looking at neglected and declining rural crafts and industries from which he developed a utopian vision of the crafts as social and economic lubricants. 'I'm really interested in the creation of interdependent pools of resources. It's sort of building on the model of old rural communities, where a single skill could be applied to various tasks. So a blacksmith might make horseshoes, barrel hoops, wheels, etc. You didn't have extreme specialist fields, but more a set of skills that could be applied to different tasks. As a designer I find that a very liberating way of thinking.'[6] This attractive vision sounds like the ruminations of an 'arts and crafter' such as C.R. Ashbee a century ago, but regrettably overlooks the necessary and inevitable specialisms of designers servicing the complex post-industrial, networked world of today.

The body of work that arose from Hasan's exploration was a series of limited edition furniture and vessels made of cleft oak, boiled leather, earthenware, steel, cast iron, bronze and brass: the materials and

techniques of vernacular craft (fig. 24). Even though Hasan's works allude to tools and objects intended for everyday use, they nevertheless belong in the gallery context (or in a book about design) and have a scent of faux-authenticity, a kind of knowing and ironic self-reference (a point made even more explicit when we compare them to Studio Job's bronze collection of rural implements called 'The Farm', to which they strongly relate). This does not invalidate them but reinforces this kind of design practice as collectible, publishable commentary rather than permissible prototypes for actual production in significant quantities.

Hasan has successfully explored various iterations of his leatherwork for galleries in New York, Paris and Milan, and for special commissions such as a reworking of Jean-Marie Massaud's 'Archibald' chair for an edition of *Wallpaper** magazine dedicated to handmade objects (2010, fig. 25). His work in leather inevitably endeared him to the Italian luxury brand Fendi, though it used his skills for promotion, rather than to design merchandise. For a while the 'design art' trend that was in the ascendant at the time Hasan established his individual practice, created a favourable context for highly individuated works in small editions, high in symbolism and 'content' but somewhat slighter in functional purpose. In hindsight, and with the retrenchment of the 'design art' market, experimental and critical works by Hasan and others take on more meaning as suggestions for reviving moribund industries using traditional wisdom: we should be looking more closely at Hasan's politics and economics concerning design's potential to reinvigorate rural industries, instead of only his works' aesthetics and symbolic value.

Industrial Facility

'I am interested in the in-between: products that are neither here nor there. Grey, rather than black or white. Products captured by people with a second glance rather than a confrontation with radicalism.'

Is Sam Hecht the best Japanese designer working in Britain today? In many respects his design preoccupations, client list, aesthetic and even one third of his studio team qualify him. Born in 1969 and educated in London, it is evident from one look that he is not ethnically Japanese. But his friendship with Naoto Fukasawa (they set up the Tokyo office of IDEO together, having met at IDEO in San Francisco), his evident love of Japanese reserve, manners, food, culture and craftsmanship, and his high-profile role as Muji's Creative Director for Europe, not to mention his collaboration with Ippei Matsumoto, senior designer at Industrial Facility, make him at least an honorary Japanese designer.

Hecht founded Industrial Facility with Californian architect Kim Colin in London in 2002, since when it has become one of the best known and most successful industrial design studios in Britain, with clients including Established & Sons (figs 29 and 30), Lexon, the Sheffield cutlers Taylor's Eye Witness, Magis and La Cie. They run the studio with a very small team of which Hecht is the spokesman. Widely published and critically acclaimed, Industrial Facility is heir to a classic era of product design epitomized by Dieter Rams and the Ulm Design School. The studio's aesthetics sometimes incorporate references to

Danish mid-century designers such as Hans Wegner, as well as the Japanese concept of 'hari' (the tautness and inevitability of design), all of which are impeccably international modern credentials.

The design critic Jonathan Glancey wrote that 'Industrial Facility is learning to shape quietude, a welcome form, and quality in a world of ever increasing visual noise',[1] and it is not just the quiet reserve of Sam Hecht, but that of his products, which encourages this view. Industrial Facility designs products that slide into the everyday landscape of use and are not intended to assault the senses, explaining their absence of ornament, colour, often even of memorable shape (a portable hard drive designed for La Cie (2007) is little more than a blank oblong, but took two years' refinement to perfect). A digital projector (2004, fig. 27) for Epson has a non-colour, 'greige' casing and is designed to slot upright into a bookshelf when not in use. Industrial Facility products deliberately fade away. As Glancey continues, 'Small, useful things, they are wholly unpretentious. There are no sudden edges. No slick ostentatious graphics. No winking lights or beeps. No ironic design games.'[2]

Hecht elaborates, 'We acknowledge that all things are dependent on each other. Rather than seeing contemporary life through an outdated Renaissance model, where everything is human-centred, self-contained and focused towards the human, instead we see that everything affects and communicates with each other, at times even independent of the human. This means seeing the world without imagining we can control it all. Imagine designing a printer or a coffee maker for the room it sits in, the table that it is on, or the person operating it. This idea allows the evacuation of superfluous functions, and the abandonment of complexity, because it acknowledges what already exists, and doesn't see a need for duplication or replication. The environment for an object, as much as its use, determines its form and content.'[3]

Hecht's holistic attitude towards products, integrating them with everyday life to imbue them with meaning and discover innate qualities, is refreshing in a sector that tends to take pride in novelty and which invented the idea of built-in obsolescence. But the same stance can make it seem that Industrial Facility is swimming against the tide. The prevailing trend in product design is for convergence of functions, and slippery terms like 'interface' predominate over old hard and fast modernist truths like 'use'. Despite this, Sam Hecht wants to 'evacuate functionality'. Compare his telephone for Muji (2003, fig. 28) to a so-called smartphone and the point is made. One can be used only to make and receive calls while the other purports to be a communication hub. The first design represents only its singular function; the second represents a portal to myriad virtual and actual places and connections.

Viewed in these terms, Hecht's reductiveness can look reactionary rather than progressive, and there persists a feeling that the 'thing itself' rather than the 'experience of the thing' is at the heart of Industrial Facility's ethos. 'Doing one thing and doing it well' is the mantra for most of its products, but that seems contrary in an age when it is quite possible for products to be multifunctional, and for consumers to be sophisticated enough to use them. Hecht's call for simplicity, reduction, calm and appropriateness is unarguable, but also largely unchallengeable.

An interesting exception to this principle is a strange but beguiling hybrid piece of furniture called 'Table, Bench, Chair' (2009, fig.29), inspired by the design of seating on the Tokyo metro, and owing much to the furniture of the Japanese-American woodworker George Nakashima (1905–1990). Hecht wrote, 'So I got to thinking ... What if there was a bench that used a chair to create a sitting zone. Then the bench would look more like a table and chair and yet still be able to act as a bench. TBC is a highly flexible matrix of different functions, where flexibility is informed by its oddity.' Surely this design is additive, not reductive, vague not specific, and its character seems to contradict other projects from the studio? Yet the ambiguity of 'Table, Bench, Chair' in part lends it the invisibility of other Industrial Facility designs. Hecht concludes: 'I am interested in the in-between: products that are neither here nor there. Grey, rather than black or white. Products captured by people with a second glance rather than a confrontation with radicalism.'[4] This is the philosophy that also informs Industrial Facility's small products for the Japanese brand IDEA International, including the 'Bell' clock (2009, a fire-alarm-style bell with a clock face) and the 'Liteplug' (2008, a combined night light and emergency torch).

Hecht is thus generally a minimalist (he did, after all, begin his career in the studio of the architect David Chipperfield), but is desire for 'less design' the same as 'no design'? The ease with which one can look past Industrial Facility's products may demonstrate just how painstakingly designed they are. In counterpoint to all this refinement Hecht and Colin delight in an anthropological approach to collecting cheap local products from their travels worldwide, as evidence of regional design solutions, all bought for 'under a fiver' (published in 2011 as *Usefulness in Small Things*). These are novelties like odd scissor/knife combinations (the failure of both in combination reinforces Hecht's commitment to reductiveness) or the curious, such as falafel scoops from both sides of the Israeli/Palestinian political divide (where design is seen as embodying some form of cultural agency). Hecht explains his intentions: 'Each object is a testament to un-global culture. Communities the world over continue to need things that serve their local needs, where design plays little or no part at all. I guess this is partly why I feel refreshed, because there is so little design as we know it today.'[5]

So does Hecht want design to play a larger cultural role, or recede into the background? Is he enamoured of localism, or a proponent of globalism? 'Globalization is about dissolution of locality. It's about forming a larger-scale economy and identity and risks the loss of a local one', he has written.[6] But is this not precisely the result Industrial Facility achieves through the creative direction of Muji, a 'no-brand brand' committed to high design values, that contrives to use a British design studio to represent Japanese cultural values to an international market?

In 2011 Industrial Facility launched its most critically successful furniture to date, the 'Branca' chair (fig. 26), manufactured by the firm of Mattiazzi in Udine, north Italy, and winner of the Brit Insurance Design of the Year Furniture Award at London's Design Museum. Until recently Mattiazzi has only manufactured for other brands, but has accrued considerable expertise and capability, including very sophisticated eight-axis computer-controlled cutting machines. It was this technology that attracted Hecht, who used it to mechanically carve chair components so fluidly and finely curved that they could almost have been moulded in plastic. Rather than conforming to usual chair-making conventions Hecht designed the chair structure, such as the seat, back and arms, to emerge as a series of branches from the legs. The enormous technical investment is downplayed in the final chair, which is well-proportioned, softly rounded, somewhat mid-century modern in character, and typically recedes into its environment rather than shouts about its presence.

In the final analysis, perhaps Industrial Facility simply assimilates a Japanese design ethos into a particularly British modern tradition. It is the quiet, rather earnest modernism that in the mid-twentieth century was associated with Gordon or Dick Russell, rather than the flash and pizzazz of their peer Wells Coates. Hecht says he identifies with 'a kind of British modernism, a modernism without the slickness, a kind of make-do-and-mend version derived from limited resources'.[7]

29. (*above*)
Table, Bench, Chair, 2009
Manufactured by
Established & Sons, UK

30. (*left*)
Two Timer clock, 2008
Manufactured by
Established & Sons, UK

Klauser and Carpenter

'Designing for me is not about trying to do something new all the time, it's about trying to do something better.'

Klauser and Carpenter combine cool, rational Teutonic modernism with more whimsical British individualism. André Klauser (*opposite, right*), born in Hanover in 1972 and trained at the Fachhochschule, Münster, brings a clear-headed, sometimes severe, austerity to the partnership, in keeping with his German industrial design background. He left Germany in 1999 to work for Jasper Morrison in London before enrolling at the Royal College of Art, from which he graduated in 2002. The highbrow product designs of Morrison and Industrial Facility are clearly inspirations to Klauser, who taught together with Sam Hecht at the Royal College of Art until 2010. British-born Ed Carpenter (born 1972, *left*) studied sculpture at Kingston University before switching to design at the Royal College of Art and establishing his own studio in 2001. Klauser describes himself as 'moody', Carpenter as 'open'.[1] Their different temperaments and backgrounds complement each other.

Carpenter's breakthrough project was the cheeky 'Pigeon' light (fig.34), an illuminated plastic bird that is more an alternative souvenir of London than a useful lamp, marketed by Thorsten van Elten since 2003. Like many of van Elten's products, it is a witty statement that marries the function of one typology to the form of another. But its clarity ensures its popularity and over 20,000 have been sold. Carpenter introduced his friend André Klauser to van Elten and together they made his first products (several designed in collaboration with Barnaby Barford), including the 'Solitaire' bowl (2003), the 'Still Life' fruit bowl (2004) and the 'Fono' Light (2006, fig.36), the first collaboration between Klauser and Carpenter. They all share van Elten's favoured ironic references to archetypal shapes and uses.

31. (*opposite*)
Utility chairs and hooks, 2009
Manufactured for Canteen by
Very Good and Proper, UK

André Klauser and Ed Carpenter share a studio in Hackney, and have an informal design partnership that allows them to work individually or together, regardless of the typology of the product. For example Klauser's powder-coated pierced steel 'Meccano' chair (2007, fig.35), inspired by the aesthetic of industrial shelving and designed for Thorsten van Elten, is his alone, but both designers claim the 'Utility' furniture (fig.31).

As have many designers of their generation, Klauser and Carpenter benefited from the advent of Established & Sons in 2005, and have completed several high-profile projects for the company, most notably the 'Louvre' light (2008, fig.33). Its angled metal louvres are an entirely functional means to direct and reflect the concealed light source, but they also give the lamp a sense of luxurious modernism.

In 2008 the pair designed the furniture for the café of the Photographers' Gallery, a leading central London venue for contemporary photographers. A second restaurant project for the London chain Canteen resulted. The constraints of designing furniture for public spaces, both in terms of performance and price, make this an exceedingly demanding market for designers. As Canteen co-owner Patrick Clayton-Malone has explained, 'restaurants have different concerns to the home when it comes to design. Things get used a lot, by lots of people. If we're doing 10,000 covers a week, that's the same tables, hooks, cutlery, being used by an enormous amount of people in a very short space of time.'[2] The first two Canteen restaurants, in Spitalfields and at the Royal Festival Hall, used furniture by BarberOsgerby, but for a new venue in Baker Street the restaurateur specified Ernest Race's aluminium BA chairs, designed in 1945, and commissioned complementary tables from Klauser and Carpenter. The Canteen tables (2009) feature aluminium legs (cast in Berlin) that can be easily attached to any tabletop. Ed Carpenter has commented, 'The BA chair was the starting point [for the leg] but it's almost too 1950s for my taste, maybe too kitsch. André and I have taken this 1950s ideal and tweaked it according to today's aspirations. Designing for me is not about trying to do something new all the time, it's about trying to do something better … We originally got the idea from the brackets in old Victorian urinals, where the casting was so beautiful. We wanted to bring this attention to detail back to a relatively mundane object.'[3] For Canteen they followed the table with the Utility chair, inspired by postwar furniture.

In the 1990s daring interior designs and furniture were a feature of London's restaurants, for example Belgo, designed by Ron Arad, or Coast, designed by Marc Newson. Canteen is a no-nonsense, no-frills British eatery, and the relative austerity of the brand and the furniture fits our more recessionary times. With Klauser and Carpenter,

32. (*opposite*)
Carina table, 2010
Manufactured by Meta, UK

Clayton-Malone founded a production business called Very Good & Proper to turn furniture commissioned for his restaurants into commercially available products, with the ethos of producing well-made, simple and pleasurable designs. The company's by-line is 'Measure twice, cut once'; sage advice from Carpenter's college tutors.

Until this point Klauser and Carpenter were concerned only with industrial design for mass production, albeit on a relatively small scale, and they have yet to work for any of the major design-led Italian manufacturers. In 2010 they took their work in another direction by designing a very expensive and exclusive table for the luxury furniture brand Meta, an offshoot of the Bond Street antique dealer Mallett's. High-profile commissions for luxurious furniture like this can greatly enhance a designer's reputation as the premium prices attract publicity and art collectors. At three metres long, the 'Carina' table (fig.32) is massive and looks like it is hewn from a single block of Carrara marble (though in fact it is cut in sections). The tables are made to order and are fabricated for Meta by Kienesberger Stein, a specialist Austrian stonemason. Supported on two slender fins, the tabletop has tapered edges giving an impression of lightness, contrary to its actual weight. The fluidity of the table's lines also seems at odds with the utility of Klauser and Carpenter's previous furniture, but by placing the narrow pedestals at right angles to one another they expose their rational design programme. Ever since Eero Saarinen's use of this material for his 'Tulip' table in 1956, monumental marble tables continue to appear unexpectedly modern, though in this instance Klauser and Carpenter have not referenced mid-century design. In recent years cutting marble with computer-aided technologies has attracted designers, among them Zaha Hadid, Amanda Levete and Sebastian Bergne, who have exploited the stone's strange propensity for fluidity. As in past centuries, marble continues to be a luxury material of choice.

These vast objects are a hybrid subset of contemporary furniture, where the material and technology seem hugely over-specified for the task and symbolism subsumes pure functionality. Though it is elegant, resolved and perfectly detailed, the luxuriousness of the 'Carina' table sits uncomfortably with the designers' preference for modest and rather austere modernism and, taking Carpenter's own success criteria, it is not clear how it is better than any marble tables that have come before it. It is formally economic, with no design eccentricities or quirks, but this is not the same as working within the tight constraints of industrial mass-production, where these designers are more at ease. The quiet detailing of the 'Utility' furniture will not make Klauser and Carpenter design-art stars, but it is ultimately more satisfying design.

33.
Louvre light, 2008
Manufactured by
Established & Sons, UK

34. (*opposite, above left*)
Pigeon light, 2003
Manufactured by
Thorsten van Elten, UK

35. (*opposite, above right*)
Meccano chair, 2007
Manufactured by
Thorsten van Elten, UK

36. (*opposite, below*)
Fono light, 2006
Manufactured by
Thorsten van Elten, UK

8

Doshi Levien

'I am trying to represent my culture in all its complexity and sophistication ... I would like to bring some of this friction and incongruity to European design.'

Those designers who come from overseas and choose to live in the UK enrich British design and culture. Immigration is both geographic and psychological, and extremes of difference between a designer's origins and Britain can lead to creative friction in their work. So too can different outlooks between design partners. In no partnership are these forces more clearly productive than in the work of Jonathan Levien and Nipa Doshi.

Doshi was born in Mumbai in 1971 but it was not until she enrolled at the Royal College of Art in her mid-twenties that she spent any length of time away from India. Her youth was far from typical because she had enrolled in the National Institute of Design in Ahmadabad when she was just 17. 'I was a girl studying furniture design and it wasn't very conducive for a woman to study such a masculine discipline. If I'd done textiles it would have been fine because all the girls studied textiles, but I studied industrial design and furniture and it was all about boys and machines and things like that.'[1] The school was founded in 1961 following the recommendations of a report on design education compiled by Charles and Ray Eames, and espouses a particularly Eurocentric, Bauhaus and Ulm-inspired modernism, at odds with the daily realities of street life outside. 'In India', Doshi has said, 'form follows celebration.'[2] She was drawn to both cultures; the formalism and utility of European modernism and the celebratory exuberance of Indian design. 'Sometimes I think I'm schizophrenic, because I love very simple utility staples and switches and German design, but at the same time I really enjoy the celebratory.'[3] Rather than being a weakness, this combination of cultural opposites, like her rejection of gender

expectations, defines her strength of personality and will. On a research visit to London in 1994 Doshi met Jasper Morrison who encouraged her to apply for the Royal College of Art.

Doshi was unsettled by her arrival in London but it afforded her a distance to critically reflect on Indian culture, and she could appreciate its strengths with fresh eyes. 'When I first came to England, I felt lost because I thought, what can I design for a culture where everything seems to already be provided for, everything is designed, what can I give? What can I design that can somehow add to this society?'[4] 'Suddenly I was in a country where everyone's needs were met. For me, design was very much about fulfilling a need or a brief. It made me look back at India and think that maybe it needs a lot of design.'[5]

Levien's background is quite different. He was born in Elgin, Scotland, in 1972 and studied cabinetmaking before attending Buckinghamshire College to study furniture design. By inclination and heritage he is a modernist (he is the nephew of the distinguished industrial designer Robin Levien). Jonathan found himself sitting beside Doshi when they joined the RCA to study product design in 1995, and recalls: 'One day she said to me, I can't be your friend if I don't respect your work.'[6] The pair graduated in 1997 but after a spell in India Doshi returned to London where she worked for SCP and the architect David Chipperfield, while Levien first went to Ross Lovegrove's studio. In 2000 they founded Doshi Levien, and almost immediately they were designing cutlery and glasses for Habitat, under the design direction of Tom Dixon.

Their breakthrough project came in 2001. During a research trip to India they had seen Tefal's European-cuisine-oriented cookware for sale. The designers contacted the French manufacturer and proposed a range of cookware specified for various regional world cuisines that would enable Tefal to penetrate those markets more effectively (fig.40). Tefal reversed the brief, preferring equipment aimed at European cooks interested in preparing cuisine from other parts of the world. Back in London, Levien and Doshi found they could research every authentic culinary tradition in their home city. The collection they designed comprised cookware for five regional cooking styles: an Indian karahi skillet, a Moroccan tagine pot, a Mexican fajita pan, a Chinese wok and a Spanish paella dish. They all featured Tefal's signature non-stick surfaces and updated traditional shapes in a contemporary idiom. Decorative patterns inspired by each region's traditions were screen-printed on their bases.

The Tefal cookware established the young practice's concern to marry regional cultural difference and industrial production that has come

82   Doshi Levien

37. (*above*)
My Beautiful Backside sofa, 2008
Manufactured by Moroso, Italy

38. (*right*)
Capo chair, 2011
Manufactured by Cappellini, Italy

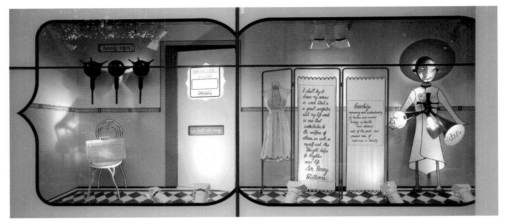

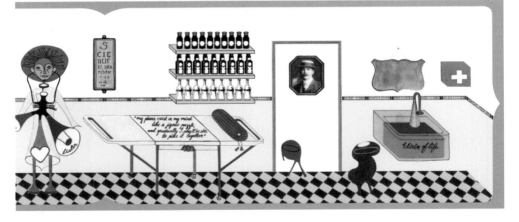

to define much of their output. The pair's individual design processes inform their work too. Typically Doshi develops her ideas through painting and collage, to which Levien applies three-dimensional structure, or, as he drily puts it, 'Nipa prefers to sit and dream and produce paintings, while I try to translate them into real life'.[7] She thinks about narrative and storytelling in two dimensions; he thinks about form and industrial processes through three-dimensional maquettes and models: each has skills that complement the other partner. 'Jonathan brings the three-dimensionality to my ideas and often it's the misunderstandings and misinterpretations that lead to the right solution. We can end up with something extra that we hadn't originally thought of. It's a one plus one equals three situation.'[8] 'Jonathan can visualize forms, and if you asked me to do that – well, I'd be at a loss. But at the same time I can do a drawing knowing that Jonathan can make something of it.'[9] Both designers share an interest in tailoring, pattern-cutting and the couture of designers such as Balenciaga, evidenced by the precision and attention to detail of their work such as the 'Paper Plane' chair for Moroso (2010) and the 'Capo' chair for Cappellini (2011, fig.38), as well as the redesign of traditional English shoes for John Lobb. 'Why does everyone want to be serious?', asks Doshi. 'Design should learn from fashion and desirability. You know, to have that sense of "pick me up".'[10]

Design should also be responsible and communicative, as in Doshi Levien's 2004 installation for the window displays of the Wellcome Trust, the London headquarters of the leading medical research charity (fig.39). Here, Doshi's whimsical miniature narrative paintings were scaled up as stage sets, with elements handmade by Indian craftsmen. The message was about a holistic approach to health care, and the paintings' colourful cartoon-like rendering of a fictional doctor's surgery ran counter to the conventional purist image of a wellbeing spa, but they enthralled passers-by.

In some respects the upholstery collections Doshi Levien have designed for Moroso elaborate on the hybrid cultures of their Tefal cookware. In Hindi 'charpoy' means 'four legs', and the 'Charpoy' sofa (2007) is a low backless divan raised on turned legs. All the visual and material focus is on the divan's pad, embroidered in an Indian factory owned by Doshi's aunt. Each divan is decorated with an image of 'chaupar', a chess-like game recorded in the *Mahabharata* and signed in thread by the embroiderers, but these are not ethnic products. The legs and frame display the quality of Italian furniture craftsmanship. The divans were accompanied by similarly decorated floor cushions called 'Tools for Inspiration', on which were applied images drawn from Doshi Levien's studio, for example Tord Boontje's 'Transglass' vases, office supplies such as staplers and even a computer fan. A three-way dialogue is therefore established between the designers in London, the craftsmen in Indian and the manufacturer in Italy.

These pieces were followed by more sofas recalling Indian history and aesthetics, and made using Indian craft skills. A miniature painting of a maharani reclining among cushions inspired 'My Beautiful Backside' (2008, fig.37), a sofa combining English tailoring and couture techniques and an Indian seating typology. The 'Principessa' sofa (2008), inspired by the tale of the Princess and the Pea, is a stack of seven mattresses, the top three of which are removable. 'There is a tribal aspect to this piece', comments Doshi. 'In areas of India mattresses are layered on top of each other every morning. So we used a really eclectic selection of fabrics and developed a red and gold jacquard weave for the top mattress.... "Principessa" is about utility and glamour.'[11] The upper-most mattress is adorned with embroidered tools for the modern princess: her sunglasses, hairdryer and umbrella.

Both partners happily concede some designs are more associated with one party than the other; Doshi's graphic and narrative proclivities are evident in these upholstered works more than Levien's form-giving. In more recent projects authorship is harder to detect. 'Kali', the four-armed Indian goddess, lent her name and her form to an innovative bathroom cabinet designed for Authentics in 2011. The Indian references are clearly from Doshi, but the pure, unadorned functionalist form is more likely Levien's. Unlike the work for Moroso, it is pure industrial design without hand craftsmanship, but the protruding Kali-arm-like shelves give character and individualism. The piece shows how Indian culture can inform a Bauhaus tradition. Doshi Levien are admired for their combination of technology, storytelling, industrial design and craftsmanship: the best of both Eastern and Western cultures. Doshi admits the stretch and the pitfalls of this ambition. 'An Indo-European design aesthetic doesn't really exist. However, what I want to challenge is the clichéd stereotyping of India, which is limited to a stylistic parody of Bollywood kitsch and curry houses. I am trying to represent my culture in all its complexity and sophistication ... I would like to bring some of this friction and incongruity to European design.'[12]

Alexander Taylor

At his best when his designs derive from two-dimensional materials folded into three-dimensional forms.

In some respects Alexander Taylor is atypical of the designers in this book. For a start he is British born and British trained, and secondly he was not educated in London. Although he maintains a studio in the capital because, he reasons, professional clients take this more seriously than an address in the regions, he chooses to live away from the London design scene, in Kent. Yet he is not a design outsider and his career has been the result of incremental expansion and development, placing him near the heart of the contemporary furniture and product design industry in Britain today.

Taylor, who was born in the north-east of England in 1975, is a graduate of Nottingham University, and began his professional career working in the London studio of architects and designers Procter Rihl (Chris Procter and Fernando Rihl). At the time, Procter Rihl were well known for their acrylic furniture, inspiring Taylor to design a chair using the material that he admits was not really intended for manufacture, but worked as a publicity vehicle. The press interest it engendered led to commissions, for example some work for the home of Alexander McQueen, and in 2002 Taylor set up his own studio. Another early break in 2003 was to be included in Max Fraser's Design UK directory together with the invitation to design something special for it. This resulted in the 'Butterfly' table comprising intersecting bent acrylic panels beneath a glass top. Taylor showed the work at the 100% Design fair in London where it was picked up by the influential Japanese manufacturer E&Y. Subsequently they disposed of the licence to Zanotta, giving Taylor his first piece of furniture to be made by a leading Italian designer. In 2004 Taylor began to design products for the London-based manufacturer Thorsten van Elten, now a firm friend, including an antler-shaped wall-mounted wire coat hook manufactured by a mattress-spring factory in the Midlands, sparking off an interest in industrial processes that continues today.

Probably Taylor's best-known product is the 'Fold' light (2005, fig. 41). At the time resistant to designing with a computer, he resolved the design of this lamp by folding paper and acrylic. An early version was included in the British Council touring exhibition *Twinkle Twinkle* and Taylor made 200 versions in anodized aluminium for an exhibition in Brick Lane during the London Design Festival. He already knew some of the team setting up the fledgling Established & Sons, which chose the lamp to be the company's very first product. Sebastian Wrong, the firm's design director, recalled: 'The reason we decided to produce the Fold light was because of its intelligent design. [It uses] a single sheet of material that is cut and bent making a functional light that has character and is economical in its use of material and utilizes modern production processes (laser cutting and sheet folding). Since launching the light we have sold many thousands of units and it continues to be an iconic piece in the collection.'[1] The first versions of the lamp were fabricated in a radiator factory in Birmingham, and subsequently Established & Sons introduced a limited edition in Corten steel for the collectors' market, as well as three sizes for general production, the smallest of which stays truest to the design concept, as it is constructed from a single folded metal sheet. The 'Fold' light won Taylor the *Elle Decoration* Young Designer of the Year award in 2005, and in the following year it gave him the distinction of being included in the permanent collection of the Museum of Modern Art in New York.

Folded metal has become a leitmotif for Taylor, who cites the sculptor Richard Serra as an influence. The 'Tank' light (2006, fig. 42), also made by Established & Sons, followed the 'Fold' light. This features 36 interlinked folded aluminium strips intended to simulate a conventional pleated lampshade, but which also contrarily evoke the heavy duty structures of military vehicles.

Another artistic influence is the work of Thomas Demand, the German artist who painstakingly constructs lifelike interiors from card and paper that he then photographs. On close inspection, the images of his interiors lack detail and perhaps it is this pared back, simplified but coherent and convincing version of modernism that we see in some of Taylor's work. Good examples could be the 'Uniform' chair (2008), inspired by utilitarian and anonymous classroom chairs, and the 'Punch' unit (2009), both designed for Established & Sons. Even the conceptual installation work of Joseph Beuys is referenced, in the 'Husky' bench for E&Y that overtly references the sledges in Beuys's *The Pack* (1969, Staatliche Museen Kassel, Neue Galerie).

Taylor seldom strays far from modernism and functional design, despite these allusions to the work of artists, and his admiration for the designs

41.
Fold light, 2005
Manufactured by
Established & Sons, UK

42.
Tank light, 2006
Manufactured by
Established & Sons, UK

of Eileen Gray and Konstantin Grcic naturally drew him towards Classicon, the Munich-based manufacturer of their works. For this firm he designed a version of the 'Butterfly' table translated into folded sheet steel, Classicon's signature material.

While almost all these works began as self-initiated projects, most have led to industrial production by leading international manufacturers. More recently Taylor has begun to work for a different sector, by designing a collection for the David Gill Gallery. Although gallery works do not need to compete with mass-produced furniture on price, the prerogative remains that they should still function perfectly. Taylor's 'Port' light and 'Cargo' table (2010, figs 43 and 44) are constructed from massive intersecting tubes, evoking both ship's fittings and heavy engineering, but with exquisite detailing. If anything, with these works Taylor's furniture is becoming more minimal, and he is at his best when his designs derive from two-dimensional materials folded into three-dimensional forms.

Is there anything particularly British about Taylor's design which is, after all, manufactured and marketed internationally? Perhaps a deep interest in the techniques of production and the traditional skills of, for example, the Midlands metalworking industries, belies a design heritage that emerged from both the Industrial Revolution and the Arts and Crafts movement, both great British innovations. The slightly off-kilter take on modernism and functionalism that gives some of this products a sense of humour and irony might also be argued to be British traits.

43. (*opposite*)
Port light, 2010
David Gill Gallery, London

44. (*below*)
Cargo table, 2010
David Gill Gallery, London

Jaime Hayon

'I'm here to tell stories with my pieces of furniture. The story doesn't have to be based on reality; it can be a complete fantasy as long as people can recognize themselves in it.'

Although the premise of this book is that it explores contemporary design in Britain, design's internationalism is a recurring leitmotif. Few designers are as genuinely international – in outlook and experience – as Jaime Hayon, a Spaniard who, since 2006, has been resident in London ('I love the diversity there, the dialogue, the hybridity').[1] Hayon's signature graphic style and his favoured materials, like ceramics and lacquered wood, express a definably Spanish aesthetic moderated by both contemporary street culture and, perhaps contrarily, top-quality traditional artisanal skills.

Born in Madrid to Spanish and Venezuelan parents in 1974, the year of Franco's death, it is tempting to see Hayon's ebullience and internationalism as symbolic of the new outward-looking post-Franco Spain. But I doubt Hayon was the easiest teenager. He was immersed in skateboard culture that gained him sponsorship from an American board manufacturer. At the tender age of 15 he began an 18-month sojourn in San Diego, California, screen-printing boards. It could have gone horribly wrong for the precocious teenager ('I couldn't speak English when I got to the States. I was like a Mexican refugee, a nobody') but rather than leading him astray Hayon's Californian interlude galvanized him to pursue a future in creativity, though he was unsure what direction to take. When he returned to Madrid, he recalled he was still 'this punk kid with no qualifications'.[2]

A series of fortunate events shaped Hayon's future. One was that Madrid's first design school was recruiting its first intake at the time of his return

to the city, and he gained a place. Naturally, skating subculture informed his work, and naturally this was at odds with the prevailing Bauhaus-inspired teaching. His narrative, graphic interests sat uneasily with conventional industrial design. By the end of his second year he ran out of money, but won a scholarship for his third year that took him to Paris to study under Philippe Starck at the École Nationale Supérieure des Arts Décoratifs, a regime he found more benign. Here he was spotted by a talent scout and offered a year's internship at Fabrica, the design think-tank-cum-hothouse near Treviso, Italy, funded by Benetton and led by its creative director, the photographer Oliviero Toscani. Hayon thrived and very quickly Toscani made him head of design. At 23 years old, he had lived in four countries, and was now leading a team of 30. For seven years Fabrica was stimulating but the young designer was increasingly distracted away from design towards management issues. Although he learned the importance of image and communication, he also questioned the design ethos. 'Form follows function belongs to the old school. In Fabrica all we talked about were concepts. I got sick of that. It was like, concepts are fine but where is the quality?'[3] Increasingly the skater boy was drawn towards hand-production techniques and traditional artisanal skills, and in 2000 he founded his own studio to pursue personal projects alongside his work at Fabrica. Hayon's first show in 2001 was 'Venezia Carnivale', comprising porcelain skittle-like figures covered in his

46. (*right*)
The Tournament
installation, 2009
Trafalgar Square, London

47.
Pixel Ballet installation, 2007
Bisazza, Milan furniture fair

signature skater graphics. He had discovered the work of Italo Bosa, a ceramicist from Borso de Grappa in the Italian Dolomites, with whom Hayon has worked on many subsequent projects.

Bosa is one of the most consistent supporters of, and influences on, Hayon, who says 'He's like my dad on the ceramics, he's just a great person'.[4] The other major influence has been Hayon's girlfriend and latterly his creative partner, the Dutch artist Nienke Klunder, photographer of many highly surreal portraits of Hayon (and of the portrait on page 95). The critic Kieran Long has recognized the importance of these images to our understanding of the designer. 'The pictures add the feeling of Hayon being a very canny operator in today's image-led design world. The portraits are in turn playful, beautiful and highly contrived. They make it clear that Hayon is far from the clichéd industrial designer working on solutions to functional problems.'[5]

Jaime Hayon's breakthrough project took place not in his adopted Italy, nor his native Spain, but in London, at the David Gill Gallery in 2003. His installation, entitled 'Mediterranean Digital Baroque' (fig. 45), 'displayed a small part of "Hayonland" that was stocked in my brain for years. Shapes and characters that had lived in my diaries for ages had a chance to come to life. Enormous ceramic cactuses accompanied by supersonic pigs, aviator pigeons and a "Hayonhome" for an army of cloned onions were only the beginning.' A visit to a cactus park in Lanzarote inspired the cactuses, made by Italo Bosa, and Hayon and his team camped out in the gallery for a week, decorating the walls with his Picasso-esque drawings. 'The entire process was exhilarating. When the space was ready to be shown, my pulse had a new rhythm. I honestly think it has been one of the greatest satisfactions of my working life. I've been hooked on installations ever since.'[6] Perhaps this is because installations inhabit a liminal space between art and design practice. 'I always work in between art and design', says Hayon. 'I don't call myself a designer or an artist, I call myself a creator. I create things, and those things are whatever you want. People love to classify but I don't believe in categories.... People need more personality. So I believe there is a moment in which design is going to be almost kitsch. Excessive. It needs personality, it needs to be more unique.'[7]

'Mediterranean Digital Baroque' introduced Hayon to an international stage that he took by storm. During the next three years he worked tirelessly and became the pin-up boy for a glamorous, Starck-inspired European narrative design-art hybrid of industrial design and craftsmanship. Commissions from Spanish firms Artquitect and BD Ediciones led him from Italy to Barcelona. For Artquitect, Hayon designed the 'AQHayon' bathroom-fitting collection, made in ceramic by Italo Bosa, in what could be described as a pop baroque style, and embellished with gold and even platinum. His innovation was to reject the notion of the bathroom as a clinical white environment separated from the rest of the home, and to design stand-alone colourful items of furniture that could, in theory, be installed in any room. Hayon's 'Showtime' furniture collection for BD Ediciones was inspired by vintage MGM musicals, and centred on the 'Multileg' cabinet (2006, fig. 48). His intention was to design a modular storage unit that did not look industrial. The cabinet features an endless parade of legs, in various traditional or invented styles. The randomness of the result is its point, as is the conscious collision between craft and industrial aesthetics. Here, in his own words, Hayon was 'providing industrialized products that are half handmade, half machined. Hybrid paella sushi!'[8]

Major commissions from mosaic-maker Bisazza for installations at the Milan furniture fair followed in 2007 and 2008. The first, 'Pixel Ballet', featured a giant Pinocchio-like figure (fig. 47); the second, 'Jet Set', was an audacious re-interpretation of a jet-fighter plane. Neither work was intended to be a prototype for functional industrially-made products but both demonstrated the deluxe character of mosaic, making them excellent communication devices for Hayon's client. His theatricality was given full vent again in the interiors for La Terraza del Casino restaurant in Madrid in 2007, and with his installation entitled 'The Tournament', in London in 2009.

'The Tournament' (fig. 47) was, in a sense, Hayon's gift to his adopted city. It took the form of a giant chess set with decoration inspired by the history of London. Hayon claimed inspiration from Lord Nelson's strategy maps, on which he planned the defeat of Napoleon's fleet in 1805, and fittingly his chess set was installed at the foot of Nelson's Column in Trafalgar Square. The Spanish designer had infiltrated to the heart of British culture and topography. Though the chess set was enormous – each piece was two metres tall, on rollers and required two 'movers' to play the game – the whole game was painstakingly handmade. Hayon worked with now-familiar collaborators Bisazza to make the board, and Bosa to craft the 32 chessmen. It may be that Hayon is just passing through London but with 'The Tournament' as the centrepiece of the London Design Festival in 2009 he has earned a place as part of British design culture.

By the end of the decade Hayon sported a long list of premium clients, among them Established & Sons, Camper, Baccarat, Moooi and Swarovski, and through his creative direction of Spanish ornament-maker Lladro he commissioned work from British-based designers Bodo Sperlein and Committee. In 2006 Emily Campbell included his work in a British

Council exhibition *My World, New Crafts* at ExperimentaDesign, in Lisbon, and commented: 'Jaime is a big personality who builds a culture around himself. But I'd never describe him as egocentric. He's one of those intellectually fearless, energetic people who dives right into the debate and is as fluent with language as he is confident with form.'[9] Perhaps his personality and life experience chime with the idiosyncratic meritocracy of British culture, where difference is valued and encouraged.

Hayon's own story so far has been remarkable. The last word is his: 'I'm here to tell stories with my pieces of furniture. The story you tell with a collection is important, because it can make it strong and coherent. The story doesn't have to be based on reality; it can be a complete fantasy as long as people can recognize themselves in it. Designers can make the world into theatre. They can make it a lot more fun.'[10]

48.
Multileg cabinet and
Showtime ceramics, 2006
Manufactured by
BD Ediciones, Spain

Troika

'If you understand design as a method, a tool, then art can be design. Art is the core, the motivation, the concept. Design is the enabler.'

The trio of designers who are Troika have complementary skills that support their practice. Conny Freyer (*opposite, centre*), born in East Germany in 1976, has a background in photography and illustration while her colleague Eva Rucki (born 1976, *left*), also German but from the west, worked in interactive media. The third member, Frenchman Sebastien Noel (born 1977, *right*), studied engineering and product design and has worked for both Ron Arad and Antonio Citterio. They met at the Royal College of Art where Rucki and Freyer studied Communications and Noel gained his MA in Design Products. Troika was founded in 2003 shortly after they graduated, supported by a grant from NESTA (the National Endowment for Science, Technology and the Arts).

With a broad skill set, both 'hard' and 'soft', two- and three-dimensional, ranging across graphics, image-making and digital media to product design and engineering, Troika is well-placed for most projects. The trio has specialized in creating spectacular kinetic installations that are both sculptural and rooted in their design disciplines, such as 'Cloud' (figs 51 and 52) and 'All the Time in the World' (fig.50), both for the British

Airways First Class Lounge at Heathrow Airport's Terminal 5 (2008). Troika contributed immersive and interactive installations to Thomas Heatherwick's 'Seed Cathedral' at the Shanghai World Expo in 2010 on the theme of the relationship between nature and urbanism in British cities (fig.49). All these high-profile projects place their work in the realm of cultural diplomacy. They are designers who do not design products, but they do write books, notably *Digital by Design* (2008), about their own work and that of their peers.

Gareth Williams: Can you say something about the idea of 'technocraft', which is a term sometimes associated with your work. I think it's about using technology – especially computers and electronics – in an individualized, non-uniform, non-industrial way. Is this a steam-punk, make-do-and-mend approach that democratizes technology because it puts it in reach of anyone capable of hacking and customizing it? In this scenario, what is the role of the professional specialist or trained designer?

Sebastien Noel: Designers and artists have always been inspired by, and responded to, scientific

and technological advances of their time. So, in this respect, art and design that use digital technologies aren't so new or different. The democratization of digital technologies is not so dissimilar to what happened to photography or graphic design 20 years ago, when photo-editing software, cheap printers and decent digital cameras became ubiquitous. Contrary to what was predicted, this was not the death of photography, nor of the professional photographers, nor of the trained graphic designer. On the contrary, I would argue that an increase in the availability of the tool has contributed to a greater general understanding of and sensibility to graphic design and photography, while the abundance of amateurs has brought new perspective to the disciplines. I believe digitally infused art and design will follow the same path, and do not think that the democratization in the availability of the tools threatens professional artists and designers. This would imply that their practice is reduced to the use of a tool, a craft in other words, which is rarely the case, the best works often transcending the mere possibilities of the medium.

Gareth Williams: You are part of a generation of practitioners trained as designers who act like autonomous artists making work that is about communicating statements more than it is about delivering functionality. Sebastien, you have said, 'We're really excited by the idea that, as artists, we can engage with commerce'.[1] Elsewhere you admitted a conflict: 'If the "Cloud" had been defined by a function, then it would have been to generate PR, or make the public see British Airways in a different way, and I think that's one of the things we need to be careful with now. If you only work with clients, there's a danger that they don't understand what you're thinking like a curator would. They will see it as a functional piece of art, and that's a danger because if you're not careful you end up making a spectacle rather than a piece of art. That's the trickiest part.'[2]

Presumably enlightened commercial patronage can enable your work, but it also brings constraints. Can you elaborate on how this affects your working practices? Does it matter whether we call your work art, public relations, advertising, design or spectacle?

Sebastien Noel: In our post-Communist world, commerce has found itself as the dominant ideology. In as much as it feels fruitful for us to deal with technology (ultimately the enabler) it is, to our eyes, highly interesting to explore the relationship art can have with commerce. Of course, commerce can provide the material support much needed by artists, but could art and design in general act as counterbalances to the commercial ideology? After all, commerce is rarely truthful, disinterested and generous.

The danger for artists is that commercial partners tend to see art or design as functional in an advertising sense: genuine, profound, engaging. It has all the apparent attributes to generate durable PR in a relatively inexpensive way. The pitfall is that commercial executives will try to control or shape the art they commission, and very often destroy its essence.

Controlling it is killing it, which in turn voids the benefits commerce was seeking there in the first place, hence the importance of educating commercial partners, and the importance of involving curators as mediators. While we understand executives will seek a return on investment (an intrinsically commercial construct) their vision and understanding of possibilities often does not extend beyond the concept of art as advertising. But advertising is a service; art isn't.

This situation rightly points towards the enlightened patronage you are describing as the ultimate working relationship between these two opposing forces. The enlightened patron is one who sees beyond the opposition,

who accepts art as art and chooses to embrace it. And since this attitude can be very successful for business too, many commercial entities try to turn towards art. From our experience, this enlightened patron is mostly very high in the hierarchy. The higher, the better, because he/she has the power to enable art, and make way for something that will be atypical and unconventional. But most of all, because he/she can often see further and beyond the obvious and direct return on investment. And yes, the resulting work will probably lie in between all the categories you are mentioning, in the sense that it will be an artwork in its own right, and will have a peripheral function as advertising. But it is important for the latter that the former is true, and that the advertising aspect remains a by-product. As a side note, and from my experience, executives' energy could be better spent on thinking how to capitalize on the piece rather than trying to influence it.

In this particular situation, there will be very little constraint on the work. But it remains a rare and privileged relationship, and one could wish to see it extended both in its occurrence and in its breadth. I am saying breadth here to include the opportunity for work that isn't only pleasing, or considered safe. Art has more to offer, but commissioning work on the darker end of the spectrum is still something extremely rare in commercial commissions, which is why we also like to work with regular galleries, where the work is accepted with fewer requirements, and virtually no constraints on the content.

Design has so far been considered only as a service with a very clear and well-defined scope of intervention. It would be interesting to explore the potential for authored design within a commercial context, and I would be curious to see the outcomes of commissioning more artistically minded designers or downright artists on classical products or services, for instance, where the manufacturer considers himself an editor of the work of a particular talent. Could this type of work happen with, say, an electronics manufacturer? After all, commerce is seeking individuality, originality and integrity. Why does it have to stop at the front door?

Gareth Williams: You have said, 'Our approach focuses on the contamination between the arts and design disciplines and is born out of the same love for simplicity, playfulness and an essential desire for provocation'.[3] Is design intended to solve problems or provoke a response? Can you 'design' an 'artwork'?

Sebastien Noel: I think it is time to acknowledge that the classical distinction between art and design is simply outdated. On one side, as you put it rightly in the previous question, there are designers who operate like artists, authoring works that escape both functionality and the classical commissioning process of design as a service to industry. On the other hand stand the contemporary fine artists who tackle topics traditionally associated with design, against theoretical backgrounds such as relational aesthetics.

What I think is more interesting in both art and design is when the outcome communicates or materializes a clear *Weltanschauung* ('world view'). I am talking here about engagement. Coming from the world of design, what I can see lacking in the discipline (and at the same time rapidly changing, which I find very positive) is a sense of responsibility towards the output, a critical understanding of the work in both a historical and contextual perspective. This is this very same self-reflection and engagement (or the lack thereof), which I think has separated the disciplines in the past. We have to remember that art and design split less than 100 years ago, and that Bauhaus teachers were very often active in both fields.

As it stands now one of the beauties of design lies in its methodology, which is why I would answer

49. (*page 105, previously*)
Green Map (*above*) and
Plant Facts & Plant Fictions
(*below*) installations, 2010
Shanghai World Expo

50. (*above*)
All the Time in the
World installation, 2008
Heathrow Airport
Terminal 5, London

51. (*above*)
Cloud installation, 2008
British Airways, Heathrow
Airport Terminal 5, London

52. (*right*)
Cloud, production process, 2008
Mike Smith Studio, London

positively to your question about designing an artwork. If you understand design as a method, a tool, then art can be design. Art is the core, the motivation, the concept. Design is the enabler.

Gareth Williams: As a contributor to the British pavilion at the Shanghai World Expo in 2010, can you say something about your experience of design in the context of cultural diplomacy? Are cultural clients so different to commercial clients, and is communicating national identity different to designing work as an adjunct of public relations?

Sebastien Noel: We found working in the context of cultural diplomacy both fascinating and highly challenging. It is mainly about communicating the values and outlook of a culture, making it understandable to a very wide audience, which in the case of the Shanghai World Expo were Chinese people with close to no knowledge about Great Britain. It also feels worthwhile, as the aim is noble, namely to better the understanding between societies. To borrow the words of William Fulbright about cultural diplomacy, 'Having people understand your thought is much greater security than another submarine'.

It is fascinating, as one needs to distill the essence of a culture, where we found we had an advantage, as none of us are British born. We believe we know the country well enough to understand the nuances of its rich and wonderful culture, yet retain the necessary distance to avoid clichés and preconceptions. This was also made easier by the presence of a theme that invited us to talk about the relationship between natural elements and British cities.

It is challenging, especially as such projects involve many high-profile stakeholders, often with different ideas about what should be communicated and how. Plus, in the case of a powerful commercial and political partner such as China, the project found itself very high on the political agenda and thus appropriately scrutinized.

For the UK pavilion in Shanghai, we were responsible for designing the visitors' experience, meaning we conceptualized and designed the exhibitions and messages presented to the visiting public as they experience the pavilion. Prior to our involvement in the project a panel of experts, the content advisory committee, was set up to ensure coherence of the overall design scheme and to safeguard the creative vision. Together with this committee and Heatherwick Studio, the architects of the pavilion, we adopted a starkly non-conformist strategy. We wanted to portray the UK as innovative, open, original and progressive. Instead of participating in the technological frenzy of the World Fairs, where many would rely on an increasing array of screens and other attention-grabbing technologies, we decided to work on creating a very peaceful and contemplative atmosphere, and relay the messages through immersive art installations. The idea was that the experience would be highly memorable, accessible and engaging, while avoiding a reliance on previous knowledge and language-based information. It meant we could also create multilayered installations, the meaning of which would automatically adapt to viewers of all ages and backgrounds.

Since the initial thinking behind the pavilion was highly atypical, working with the Foreign Office wasn't so dissimilar to working for commercial clients, and the content advisory committee had to both explain and reassure that the project's approach would be interesting and fruitful, which it ultimately was, the UK pavilion having been voted the visitors' favourite pavilion, and awarded the Gold Medal by the Chinese Authorities.

Of course, since this type of project resulted in art installations, it had a strong communication agenda, and we believe it to be a very successful example of fruitful symbiosis between art and design disciplines.

rAndom International

'We believe there should be poetry in the mass-produced object. We believe that the digital is best experienced in tangible, analogue ways. We believe that raw simplicity communicates complex ideas best.'

'I think digital media will have a much more physical quality in future', says Hannes Koch (*opposite, left*), one third of rAndom International and the team's most vocal spokesman. 'Lighting could be activated by gesture-recognition with a space "reading" your body movements, for example. We're laying the ground with our designs but you'll soon see it coming through in commercial products.… Which is a good thing because we need to bring body and soul into technology and put a smile on people's faces.'[1]

In this single statement Koch summarizes his design preoccupations. Digital technology's abstract and virtual character is soulless, yet its human users want more emotional relationships with it. The designers' works might be experimental, experiential and bespoke, but they are actually predictors of the near future of product design. Koch frequently describes rAndom International as 'media artists', indicating not only their communicative intentions but also the existence of their works in limited editions, performances and museum and gallery contexts.

British design education brought these partners together. Only Stuart Wood (born 1980, *right*) is British, the other two designers, Hannes Koch (born 1975) and Florian Ortkrass (born 1975, *centre*) are German. They met at Brunel University in west London studying Product Design and Industrial Design Engineering, and formed rAndom International

in 2002 before all joining the Royal College of Art the following year, Koch and Ortkrass to study Design Products while Wood joined Anthony Dunne's Design Interactions department. On graduation in 2005 they immediately set up their studio in Brixton, latterly extended with a Berlin office.

At first the designers thought they were working at the cutting edge of product design development, and certainly their work derives from the debates around mass production, functionality, technology and efficiency. Often it was the process that fired their imagination without having a commercial outcome in mind, for example the 'Temporary Graffiti' pens and 'Pixel Rollers' (both 2005), which combined digital imaging technology, light sources and luminous inks. Koch makes the 'Pixel Roller' sound simple. 'You take a digital image, you put it in a computer. And then you use this device we came up with to print it out in one go onto a canvas or on a wall. So it's an immediate way of hand painting. And we did this with light as well.'[2] The apparent simplicity is an important part of rAndom International's practice, which they defined in a manifesto published in 2007. 'We believe there should be poetry in the mass-produced object. We believe that the digital is best experienced in tangible, analogue ways. We believe that raw simplicity communicates complex ideas best.'[3]

The active performances that characterize these early works define them, as do a preoccupation with portraiture and reflection that served to humanize the digital technologies. The designers performed with their designs to demonstrate works like the 'Pixel Roller', and later they developed more autonomous objects such as a series of 'Temporary Printing Machines' (2007, see fig.53) that did not need them in attendance, but which nonetheless relied on an intimate relationship between spectator and object, played out through a brief moment in time. With 'Audience' (2008, fig.54), rAndom International combined advanced digital technology and human behaviour.

'Audience', a collaboration with the digital artist and designer Chris O'Shea, was commissioned by the choreographer Wayne McGregor. It comprises 64 mirrors, each the size of a large book, mounted close to the floor on computer-driven motorized stands that allow them to twist and turn. Though utterly technical in appearance, in character they are each cartoonish and vaguely zoomorphic, especially as they are programmed to turn randomly to each other in a state of apparent chatter. When a visitor steps into their field they are sensed by a camera, and as one the mirrors turn to face him or her, confronting the spectator with a multitude of their own reflection. The mirrors will continue to follow this person as they move, until they appear to lose interest and

54.
Audience installation, 2008
Royal Opera House, London

chat together, or seek another person to focus upon. The audience of the title is both the assembled mirrors and the spectators who view them, each performing for the other.

The project may have begun as a performance commission as well as applied design research exploring our relationship with technology, but it resulted in an edition of eight installations for the Carpenters Workshop Gallery, London. The support of enlightened galleries and other patrons is essential for the success of speculative design work such as this. Like Troika, rAndom International is unafraid of commercial collaborations if they enable their projects. A good example is a project first shown at the Milan furniture fair in 2009 called 'You Fade to Light'. This was initiated by electronics giant Philips who wanted to explore and promote the potential of its new OLED light modules. Unlike conventional LEDs that give a sharply focused light, organic light-emitting diodes create a uniform soft and dispersed light. Lighting supremo Ingo Maurer dislikes them ('OLED lighting is even and monotonous. It has no drama; it misses the spiritual side'), but rAndom International were attracted to their 'almost unreal' quality of light.[4] They attached together a panel of more than 1,000 OLED modules that responded to a spectator's movement and reflected it back in terms of light and darkness. OLED modules are more familiarly encountered in mobile phone interfaces and lighting, and 'You Fade to Light' was an attempt to humanize and visualize technology that is becoming seamlessly embedded in products and environments. Koch explains the role of designers like rAndom International. 'We see there is an increasing demand [for] work that makes technological or scientific concepts more approachable. A lot of the things we use in our day-to-day life are becoming less and less tangible, and people really seem to prefer experiencing something to just understanding it. On a practical level, it's of course a designer's role to design interfaces and interactions that help the user to engage with an object. Media artists can be a little less practical but essentially often have the same role, in that they can create pieces that help to fulfil the increasing demand for a critical or surprising answer to a lot of questions that many seem to share.'[5]

In 2010 rAndom International were named Designers of the Future by the Design Miami/Basel fair, another incidence of commercial patronage of emerging hybrid design practice. In Miami they showed a new work entitled 'Swarm' (fig.55), once again completed with the Carpenters Workshop Gallery. 'Swarm' is ostensibly a chandelier, in that it hangs from the ceiling and emits light, and in this sense it is the most conventional project to date for the designers. Yet it is also the most technically complex and variable. Whereas 'You Fade to Light' and the 'Temporary Printing Machines' responded to the presence of a spectator in two dimensions, 'Swarm' added a third dimension. Koch explains that it was inspired by the swarming behaviour of insects like bees and flocking birds such as starlings that appear to gain group intelligence. 'It's probably somehow explicable. But it's incredible. Because of the efficiency of movement. And the sheer economy of movement. And the beauty of it. I think that a lot of people instinctually find it very ecstatic, and very beautiful, very elegant in its form. That such a number of individual objects can move in conjunction without colliding, without chaos, without crashing.'[6] For their 'Swarm', the designers constructed cubic light grids, each composed of 144 LEDs, programmed to appear animated by a swarming cloud of light. The swarm may scatter or flow away from sudden noises, such as the clapping of hands, so the work is also responsive to its audience. Like 'Audience' it has a non-specific zoomorphism derived from representation of animal behaviour rather than physiognomy.

The designers of rAndom International seldom design anything that we may describe as a product, but their work lives alongside product design and digital technology, pointing the way forward for both. They are technical marvels but they are humanized by our interaction with them. As Koch concludes, 'Most of our pieces only really work when you are there. You complete them. Without you being there they are just pretty, or aesthetic, but don't have any deeper meaning.'[7]

13

Moritz Waldemeyer

'Often with technology there doesn't seem to be any limit, which is amazing. It means anything is possible.'

Moritz Waldemeyer (born 1974) has been described as 'the design world's engineer-for-hire' and 'the expert's expert'.[1] He is a highly skilled enabler for other designers and represents a trend in contemporary design practice away from designing products for the market and towards designing extremely technical experiences and installations. We might say the same for a number of designers in this book, but the difference with Waldemeyer is that he is principally an engineer who has come into the world of design, firstly as a technician enabling the ideas of designers (some of whom are in this book) and latterly as a designer and 'auteur' in his own right. His presence at the forefront of new design practice is testament to both the specialism and the hybrid nature of contemporary design.

To elaborate: as digital technology and information proliferate exponentially it is inevitable that very specialized technicians such as Waldemeyer will emerge to service the intentions and ambitions of those designers who cannot master all techniques. For example, it was Waldemeyer who worked out the mechanism to make Fredrikson Stallard's monumental 'Pandora' chandelier (fig.60) appear to fragment and re-materialize. Secondly, the ways in which these technologies cross between conventional disciplines, from product design to communications and fashion, demonstrates a hybrid state where anything is possible and practitioners can move freely across genres.

Waldemeyer's specialism is 'mechatronics', which he describes as 'simply a combination of mechanics and electronics. It's a relatively new discipline, but almost everything we use nowadays – a washing machine, the electric windows in a car – is automated in one way or another.'[2] The son of doctors in the former East Germany, Waldemeyer initially came to Britain to

56. (*opposite, above*)
Dress, 2007
Hussein Chalayan,
One Hundred and
Eleven collection,
Spring/Summer 2007

57. (*opposite, below*)
Dress, 2007
Hussein Chalayan,
Airborne collection,
Autumn/Winter 2007

study business but he discovered 'mechatronics' on a university trip to a Bosch plant in Virginia, and later enrolled at King's College, London, to specialize in the subject. From there he spent a spell at Philips in the Netherlands working on research and development projects before setting up his own studio back in London.

An early breakthrough came when Waldemeyer cold-called Ron Arad to offer his services. Arad asked him to work on 'Lolita' (fig.58), a digital chandelier for an early Swarovski Crystal Palace collection presented in Milan in April 2004, for which Waldemeyer provided the technical know-how for a text message sent from a mobile phone to appear as illuminated text moving along the ribbon-like crystal structure. Working with Arad on this and other pieces gave Waldemeyer great exposure, and over the next few years he contributed to several interactive objects for the Swarovski project, including 'Voyage' for Yves Béhar (2005) as well as 'Pandora' for Fredrikson Stallard (2007).

It could be said that Waldemeyer contributed as much to the success of these projects as the designers or Swarovski, because his technical virtuosity enabled their visions. More than 60 designers have contributed work to the Crystal Palace collection, some with several designs, since Tord Boontje's paradigm-shifting 'Blossom' chandelier launched it in 2002. Through this project undeniably Swarovski has become a major patron of a certain type of contemporary design: the bold, the extravagant and the eye-catching, in keeping with the character of the company's core product and the luxury market sector in which it resides. It is easy to be critical of Swarovski as a patron if your definition of worthwhile design does not include the luxury sector, but Waldemeyer is careful not to bite the hand that feeds him. When asked about Swarovski's contribution to design he replied: 'I think they have taken on an amazing role of being the ultimate patron of the arts because they have poured incredible amounts of money into design. At the same time with all that freedom they could do a lot better. They should be more courageous, in some ways they do play too safe.'[3] To a degree, the caution Waldemeyer perceives seems at odds with the extraordinary objects using cutting-edge technology that the Crystal Palace project has engendered.

To date, Waldemeyer's longest lasting collaborative project has been with the fashion designer Hussein Chalayan (figs 56 and 57), yet Chalayan does not acknowledge Waldemeyer as more than a technician. For his part, Waldemeyer clearly relishes his involvement in this sector. Chalayan's conceptual and futuristic fashion vision gives free rein to Waldemeyer's technical imagination. 'I love taking elements from the fashion work and turning them around somehow to make something

58. (*below, left*)
Lolita chandelier, 2004
Ron Arad for Swarovski
Crystal Palace collection

59. (*below, right*)
By Royal Appointment
chairs, 2007
Gallery Libby Sellers, London

60. (*opposite*)
Pandora chandelier, 2007
Manufactured for Swarovski
Crystal Palace collection
From left: Patrik Fredrikson,
Ian Stallard, Moritz Waldemeyer

new', says Waldemeyer. 'And often with technology there doesn't seem to be any limit, which is amazing. It means anything is possible. It doesn't feel like rocket science at all.'[4] Waldemeyer has contributed to collections featuring lasers and crystals; dresses that performed as video screens; and most spectacularly, kinetic dresses that transformed their silhouette, one even vanishing into the rim of the model's hat.

Many designers in this book incorporate performance and explore the theatrical potential of technology. In conclusion, Waldemeyer's work offers a new paradigm for designers where digital technology becomes the design medium itself, rather than merely the tool to achieve an end, or the appliance of design engineering in the service of aesthetics. He envisages an integrated future, where the digital and the analogue are fully united and dematerialized. He has tried this with works such as 'By Royal Appointment' (2007, fig.59), a series of high-backed chairs made for Gallery Libby Sellers embedded with technology to detect the colour of a sitter's clothing and project a corresponding light aura around them. The 'Disco' table designed specially for *Wallpaper** magazine included an iPod dock, smoke machine and lasers to create a domestic dancing cage. But these designs are formally unsophisticated and Waldemeyer's best work remains in the integration of digital controls, light and video with stage clothes for acts as diverse as OK GO, U2, Rihanna and the Black Eyed Peas. In the twinkling limelight world of show business, Waldemeyer's 'mechatronics' make perfect sense.

Simon Heijdens

'I try to reintroduce the time factor into environments or objects that were conceived to be static. This is because I can't help thinking that an absence of elements able to give back sense to the evolution of things, and therefore to their history, is a loss.'[1]

Simon Heijdens's resistance to categorization makes it seem all the more pertinent to try to determine where he fits in. He purports to dislike being defined as an interaction designer, preferring the term 'ambient designer', even though his digital light projections often interact with their viewers and environments. Arguably Heijdens's training classifies him as a product designer: he graduated from product and media design at Design Academy Eindhoven in 2002. But he also studied experimental film-making at UdK Berlin (Universität der Künste/University of the Arts). His *modus operandi* is often the moving image: does that make him a film-maker or animator? But is he actually a digital artist or a 'gallery designer' working in the realm of 'design art' because he uses cutting-edge digital technology to create site-specific installations? Do these distinctions help or confuse us?

The best definition of Heijdens's work may be that it is digital, space-specific, performance-based and uses time as a medium, but this could equally be said of various projects by Troika, Moritz Waldemeyer and rAndom International. Heijdens specializes in using computer

software to create immersive experiences, and these are often situated in commercial galleries, art fairs, design festivals and museums. Since the public, commercial and institutional interest in emerging design practices, including digital experiments, has gained momentum in recent years it is possible for practitioners like Heijdens to thrive on this international circuit.

Heijdens was born in Breda in the Netherlands in 1978, and moved to London in 2005. Unlike many other designers discussed here, he did not study at the Royal College of Art, but has tutored there. His reasons for coming to London are familiar: 'I came here in 2005 as it's a very different and interesting city to live and work in. It's becoming a central point in the world where things pass through and the input is fantastic. There's amazing exhibitions and so much to see, but at the same time it's exhausting to do all these things.'[2] To Heijdens London seems both specifically itself but also connects everywhere, and is at once stimulating and enervating. I am reminded of Marc Augé's 'non-places' like international airports that are both self-evidently located, and appear to be bland, placeless and identical.

Specificity of site re-occurs in Heijdens's work in peculiar and contradictory ways. His ambition is to re-introduce nature into the synthetic man-made modern world and for light projection works such as 'Tree' and 'Lightweeds' (fig. 61), both conceived in 2005, he wrote digital code to generate simulations of flora (trees, weeds) that appear to 'grow' according to the random influences of their environments. Because the plant forms are entirely generated by data that is moderated by apparently unpredictable forces, Heijdens does not think of these as animations so much as evolutions.

The trees are projected eight metres high on to buildings and sensors record environmental data that Heijdens translates into appropriate motion for the simulated tree: on windy days, for example, his trees appear to thrash in the wind. In this sense they are specific to their sites, but Heijdens has projected ostensibly identical digital trees (clones arising from identical original data) with remarkably similar results, in cities across Europe, Asia and North America, seemingly contradicting their site specificity. Further sensors translate loud noises, or the motion of passers-by, into digital commands for the tree to shed its digital leaves. These stimulations are not analogous to nature's processes such as wind or seasonal change so Heijdens has introduced an unnatural connection between the action and the result. On falling, the projected leaves gather in drifts on the street and, like real leaves, respond to breezes and passing pedestrians. At the end of each day Heijdens's trees are denuded, but a drift of projected leaves illuminates the street below. It is a poetic

62. (*opposite*)
Shade installation, 2010
Art Institute of Chicago

analogy for nature's cycles of growth and decay and Heijdens calls the project 'a fake forest revealing real nature', also reminding us that little about the landscape of his native Netherlands is natural, including the trees on the street.[3]

The 'Lightweeds' projections are a more sophisticated evolution of the 'Tree' project. Heijdens retained sensors to record the weather conditions outside but here the projections take place indoors. Now, weed-like plants appear to grow up the walls, flower, pollinate and spread to new parts of the building: another evocation of nature's cycles. He first installed it at a hospital in Rotterdam, where its context was 'art therapy', but the project has also been shown in a gallery context by Libby Sellers in London (2008), who described its effect as like 'a visual lullaby – like sitting in an organic field all day long. Beautiful and peaceful'.[4] As with 'Tree', the 'Lightweeds' show signs of growing rather indiscriminately worldwide, the latest iteration being in Salt Lake City (2011). Critic Janice Blackburn imagined 'the soothing influence it might have in my home – far more interesting than conventional wall coverings or the self-conscious artistic presence of a video installation'.[5] While she may be emphasizing the commercial and decorative potential of the project, and was predicting its impact as an element of domestic interior design, Blackburn was not unaware of Heijdens's more philosophical intentions, inspired by George Perec's book *Species of Spaces* (1974) in which he wrote, 'People have to forget there are walls but have found nothing better on which to hang up paintings. Paintings erase walls, but after a while the walls will kill the painting, for the painting becomes the wall. One has to either always change painting or wall'.[6] With 'Lightweeds', Heijdens reinvented the notion of framed picture, decorated wall, fixed image and solid surface. A third iteration, 'Branches', shown in London and Design Miami/Basel by Gallery Libby Sellers in 2010 (fig.63), creates on an indoor ceiling an impression of dappled sunlight through a leafy canopy. Once again the motion of the leaves and boughs is controlled by sensors outside the building, and evokes the real weather conditions. Heijdens claims all these projects are about dissolving the unnatural boundaries imposed by architecture, and letting back in the nature we have walled out. To an extent this holds true, but perhaps the trees, plants and leaves are too literal and figurative, and too synthetic, graphic and mathematical to capture nature as Heijdens wishes. If his aim is to reveal nature, why not work more directly with botany or horticulture? Other digital designers have taken more abstract approaches to simulating nature, with more compelling results, for example the light work 'Swarm' by rAndom International.

Some museums have played pivotal roles in promoting and developing emerging design practice, not least the Museum Boijmans Van Beuningen

63. (*opposite*)
Branches installation, 2010
Gallery Libby Sellers
Andaz Hotel, London

64. (*below*)
Café installation, 2009
Museum Boijmans Van
Beuningen, Rotterdam

in Rotterdam, which was quick to embrace the wealth of local design talent. In 2009 the museum gave over the redesign of its front of house facilities to a team of designers calling themselves 'Haunting Dogs, Full of Grace', comprising Simon Heijdens, Ted Noten, Frank Bruggeman, Wieki Somers, Jurgen Bey and Bertjan Pot. Heijdens contributed an espresso bar (fig.64) and commented, 'Where the museum curates its art collection, the espresso bar curates its visitors'.[7] He installed cameras above each table to capture text from any literature laid on them by visitors, and then converted this data into ever-changing disks of text pattern projected on to the ceiling. In this way the museum's visitors were able to affect the shape and content of the work. They could even take it away as a souvenir, as fragments were also printed on their till receipts. The absence of simulated nature does not reduce the impact of this work, which in this case is site-specific and appropriate.

With 'Shade' (fig.62), installed on the windows of the Art Institute of Chicago's Modern Wing in 2010, Heijdens abandoned figuration in favour of an abstract representation of nature. Here, a responsive film applied to the window glass darkens segments of a triangulated pattern in accordance with the stimulation received by wind and light sensors outside. This causes the light inside to be in constant flux and modulation. Abstracting, rather than simulating, nature appears to have liberated Heijdens's practice.

Onkar Kular and Noam Toran

'Every object is a "screen" on to which we project use, affection, anger, desire, freedom.'

Onkar Kular (born 1974, *opposite, left*) and Noam Toran (born 1975, *right*) do not design products for the mass market, or indeed for any market. In fact, little of their time is spent designing anything that could be taken to be products or objects at all. They spend considerably longer researching, writing and thinking about the nature of design and about the roles taken by designed objects in culture and society.

It should be said that even though they appear here together, they often work alone. Both of them teach at the Royal College of Art (where they also studied), but they have very different backgrounds. They make rather an odd couple: Toran was born in New Mexico to Eastern-European Jewish stock, while Kular is a British-born Sikh from Huddersfield. The collision between these varied cultural, racial and national personal origins in their collaborations may also be the source of a consistent theme in their work: the differences between the 'real' and the 'unreal', or the search for authenticity. Reflecting on these themes, Anthony Dunne (who taught them both and now employs them to teach his Design Interactions course at the RCA) observes that, in Western societies, 'there is one place for the "real" real and another for the "unreal" real. The former exists in the here and now, while the latter lies behind glass screens, within the pages of books and locked in people's imaginations.' Perhaps this is another way of speaking of the range of design practice from industrialized commodity to critical commentary. Dunne continues, 'For as long as I've known Onkar, he's been fascinated by popular culture (especially celebrity culture), and using design to overcome the invisible but solid walls separating dreams and imagination from everyday life'.[1] Toran's love of cinema, the ultimate modernist simulation of reality, underlies his analysis and deconstruction of cinematic tropes.

How do the themes of celebrity culture and cinema play out in their work? In 2008 Kular investigated the entertainment industry (his research was funded by Tussauds Studio, a visitor attraction company).

Onkar Kular and Noam Toran

He recalled the childhood moment he realized his televised wrestling heroes, Big Daddy and Giant Haystacks, were locked in staged, not real, combat. 'Maybe in the back of my mind I already knew what I was watching was not really authentic, sitting in what I would now describe as the indefinable space between reality and fiction.'[2] Kular concluded his chief interest was how the designed elements of backdrop, costume, even script, contribute to an effect, and the major outcome of his project was 'Elvis Was Here', a day-long workshop with schoolchildren, collaborating with Paul Ritchie, an established Elvis impersonator. The minimum requirement to be an impersonator is to look like, act like and sound like your subject, so through observation and imitation the schoolchildren were able to become like Elvis, and in so doing explore definitions of impersonation, identity and authenticity, culminating in a rousing performance of 'Hound Dog' for fellow pupils. Although far from being a tangible product, this has everything to do with design as we can easily consider the construction of Elvis's identity as a combination of designed outcomes, from his rhinestone cape to his curled lip. The exercise invites us to reflect upon the role design plays in constructing personal, or alternative, identities and reconnects to the prevailing theme of performance as a tool of the design process that we have encountered through much of this book.

Toran is also concerned with design and performance: 'Often in my work, I foreground objects as protagonists in a narrative that I then film.'[3] He has developed this through a series of short films such as 'Object for Lonely Men' (2001), in which the protagonist re-enacts scenes from Jean-Luc Godard's 'Breathless' using props arranged on a tray, and 'Desire Management' (2006), featuring ambiguous uses of real and imagined domestic appliances such as a vacuum cleaner and a device to catch tears. The role of designed objects in forwarding and defining the cinematic narrative is paramount, but nonspecific and open to question.

Kular and Toran have collaborated on an ambitious project to compile all the death scenes in the history of cinema. The first instalment, 'Proposal for an Impossible Library' (2007, fig. 66) divided the death scenes from 150 films into categories, such as 'Dying in Bed', 'Dying while Singing' and 'Dying in Arms'. The film was commissioned by the Wellcome Trust as part of a project studying the fine line between life and death.

The designers have collaborated on two further major projects in recent years. Probably led by Toran's cinematic interests they developed a fascination for what the film director Alfred Hitchcock described as 'MacGuffins', objects that recur throughout a film, upon which the plot rests but which are not necessarily intrinsic to it. For example, in film noir MacGuffins might be sets of keys, rolls of microfilm or attaché cases. In 2008 Kular and Toran conceived the 'MacGuffin Library', an ongoing project to create a library of objects together with short written film scenarios melding fact and history, fiction and imagination (fig. 65). According to Toran, 'Some of the objects are "mundane" objects; they are pre-existing objects and we are providing them with this sort of value and importance through the narrative. Other objects have been designed specifically for the purpose: we have created them and worked with engineers and sculptors to get them made just the way we want.' The text and object are contingent on each other and 'although we are not making the film we are hopefully producing space between the object and the synopsis where an audience can create the film themselves, and where they can think of what we are intending to present cinematically'.[4] Crucially, all the objects were made using rapid prototyping as exact simulations of the real thing, adding a layer of fiction and further blurring the boundaries of 'real' and 'fake'. In 2008 the project was presented in a laboratory setting as part of an exhibition in the Embankment Galleries at Somerset House, London, entitled *Wouldn't it be Nice... Wishful Thinking in Art and Design*.

The second major collaboration between Toran and Kular was even more ambitious and drew on many now-familiar themes in their work. 'I Cling to Virtue' (fig. 67), staged in a disused gallery at the V&A in 2010, was nothing less than a melding of cinematic and literary conventions with personal, social and universal historical themes, expressed through a series of designed objects. More than any other designers in this book, Toran and Kular show a sophisticated understanding of the ways in which objects can act as 'psychological vessels'. 'Every object is a "screen" on to which we project use, affection, anger, desire, freedom', explains Toran. 'For us, what adheres to an object is much more important than what it "is".'[5]

The exhibition's conceit was that it was curated by a fictional character, Monarch Lövy Singh, using objects from his family's history since the early twentieth century. Kular and Toran created a timeline drawing on their own emigrant/immigrant family histories that created fictional ancestors for Monarch as well as recording national and international events as a context for their lives. Then, as with the 'MacGuffin Library', they created facsimile objects accompanied by snippets of text that combine to create cinematic snapshots alluding to universal themes. It is an audacious and highly original working method that steps far beyond the regular confines of design practice, but builds upon our understanding of objects as cultural signifiers. The objects are often mundane: spectacles, a videotape in an envelope, or a child's tricycle, with apparently little to connect them. Kular and Toran demand that we, the audience, enter their fictional space to decode their meaning, which can be deduced or supposed from the Raymond Carver-esque text vignettes that accompany the objects. But everything is ambiguous because 'memory is never in perfect control of what it preserves, and a memoirist is largely a fiction-maker', as we are told by Lövy Singh/ Toran/Kular in the introduction to the exhibition text.

Once again the objects were fabricated using three-dimensional printing, this time in chalk-white resin. He/they continue: 'because the real objects of memory vanish the longer we stare at them, the objects tied to the stories I tell take the form of blanks or voids, white as ghosts.'[6] The objects are all immaculate digitally reproduced facsimiles, simultaneously individual and universal, ephemeral and eternal, at the juncture of anthropology, model-making and conceptual art, that perform as sculptures of designed objects. As far from the interests of the 'design-art' market as they are from the constraints of designing for industrial production, these objects present a compelling new direction for design culture.

66. (*below*)
Proposal for an Impossible
Library, film stills, 2007

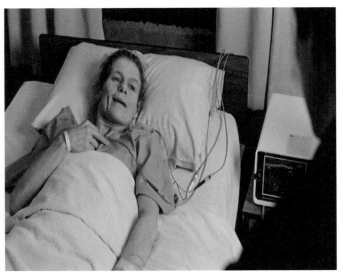

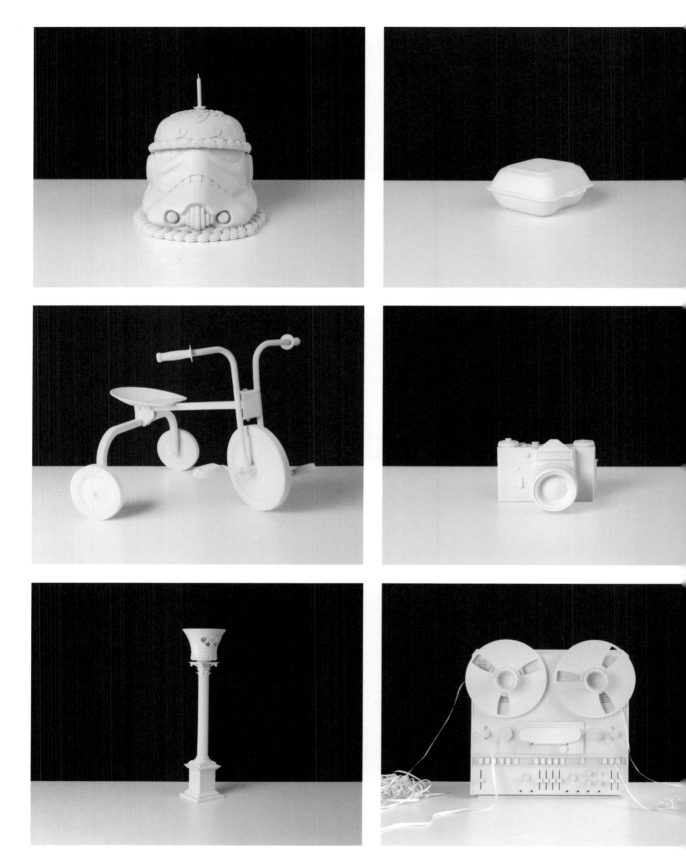

67. (*opposite and below*)
I Cling to Virtue
installation, 2010
The Victoria and Albert
Museum, London

Julia Lohmann

'I always want to go one step beyond what is naturally comfortable.'

Julia Lohmann (born 1977) is a German designer who graduated from the Royal College of Art in 2004 and now divides her time between Hamburg and the British capital. Her work is sometimes contentious and challenging, and she does not shy away from confronting moral or ethical issues in her products and objects, which are generally made in small numbers and presented through galleries. An initial interest in animals, and in products made from them, led to several widely published designs, including lamps made from preserved cow and sheep stomachs ('Ruminant Bloom', 2004, fig. 68), a stool cast from the organ cavity of a calf ('Lasting Void', 2007, figs 71 and 72), and benches cast from soap ('Erosion', 2007), some of which she completed in collaboration with her husband, Gero Grundmann, a graphic designer. More recently Lohmann's interests have broadened into an exploration of less obvious natural resources such as seaweed as materials for products ('Kelp Constructs', 2008, and 'Laminarium', 2010, figs 73 and 74).

Gareth Williams: You have often said that your work is about raising awareness of the material sources for products, most notably by drawing attention to our relationship with animals. For example, 'I've always been interested in the transition of an animal to a product. The transition point is not the killing, or when you take the organs out – we still have emotions for the animal then. It's only when it's cut up that it becomes steak and we feel detached. I wanted to capture this moment of transformation.'[1] Why is design the best means of exploring this transition from life to death?

Julia Lohmann: When communicating through objects the meaning is created through the materiality of the object. The materials become words; the design becomes the syntax. The piece speaks without the detour of language.

Communication through objects triggers an emotional response that circumvents language and its pitfalls. By staying in design, anchored in consumer society and interwoven with everyday existence the thoughts my objects carry have access to peoples' lives 'through the back door'. When people read about my 'Cow Bench' as a sofa they immediately imagine it in their living room, imagine how it would feel to sit on it, how it would fit into their everyday surroundings. They immediately relate it to a place right in the middle of their lives and even if my objects aren't handled and consumed in the same way as mass-produced items, they are still understood in the context of design and have that directness.

My overarching message is not just about animals. My message is that objects communicate their story and that it is important for us to engage with this. This communication includes the

materials and the processes by which they were produced. My work is about the stories objects tell and the ethical responsibility they transfer. I want people to read objects differently, to ask more questions about them, to learn to read their objects beyond brand values and functionality and to engage with them with an inquisitive mind.

Gareth Williams: Wouldn't it be more effective to use words and language rather than objects and design to draw attention to these issues? You already use the language of activism, for example, 'Whether or not to go vegetarian is a personal choice – but it's a choice everyone should make actively. Our relationship with animals is not a simple yes or no debate. Acknowledging the origins of a product is a first step towards making more ethical choices about what we consume.'[2]

Julia Lohmann: Language involuntarily plays a huge role in disguising production processes: salmon are called salmon, whether they are wild fish or farmed. Why are they called by the same name? Salmon farmers have profited hugely from the air of luxury surrounding the fish but have very quickly eroded this reputation. A chicken pie is called by the same name whether it is a heavily processed supermarket-bought item made from factory farmed chicken, hydrogenated fats and preservatives or a handmade home-baked pastry with the leftovers from the Sunday roast. This is eroding the ability of language to denote quality, it is eroding the relevance of names and it is disabling the consumer from distinguishing one item from the other.

Animals are omnipresent in our lives. They used to appear as food, prey or predators. Now they have moved more and more into the realm of the artificial; their names have been used to denominate toys, cartoons, posters and human qualities. Animals are still omnipresent but only as representations that carry the same name as the real creatures. It is as if they have started new anthropomorphized lives of their own, made to distract us from our loss of the real thing.

The 'Snow White' mice (2006) are a way of illustrating and communicating this point. I set out to connect some extreme and even contradictory ideas of 'mouseness' in a single object, by combining the 'Disneyfied' kitsch porcelain mouse that is ubiquitous today with the shape of a real mouse classed as snake food and available in shock-frozen packs of 12 in pet stores. Linguistically many different animals, creatures, concepts and ideas are grouped together under one name: mouse. The process of designing and making the 'Snow Whites' transforms the object from one extreme, snake food, into the other extreme, a kitsch jewellery mouse. It still retains the features of the original animal and is closely linked with its origin through its mode of production. The process is like a time-lapse film of how the image of a mouse has changed in our heads over time. Whereas it is difficult to communicate this in real time, the design process compresses it into a time frame and the object can be accessed and understood intuitively.

Gareth Williams: Is there a difference between experimenting with materials to explore their formal properties, and experimenting with ideas to find the most effective way of communicating? Which came first: your interest in animal parts as prospective materials, or your realization that intrigue and shock could get your audience thinking and provoke a response? For example, you can't have been surprised visitors were initially disgusted by your dyed maggots, when you provocatively showed them at Tate Modern ('Maggotypes', 2001, fig.70). Presumably their shock was your desired outcome.

Julia Lohmann: For the projects I have done with animals, the question 'what came first?' was the realization of an absurd situation and is something I asked myself. I question my own actions and decisions that are based on

68. (*above*)
Ruminant Bloom light, 2004

69. (*right*)
Tidal Ossuary, 2010, with
Gero Grundmann
Gallery Libby Sellers

my cultural and societal background. I question whether my socialization is based on values and beliefs that I can agree with. If I question my own actions, based on society's values, the questions will also relate and communicate well to others.

As for shock, this is mostly for my own benefit as well, to enable me to snap out of what I take for granted and to have a moment when I can rethink and go back to first principles. That is what I would like others to do as well. So I am not setting out to design for shock, but to go back to square one and to free myself and the people who see and use my work from what we take for granted. With each project I am pushing myself and I am as demanding of myself as I am of others.

The reason I enlisted the maggots was to challenge myself. I always want to go one step beyond what is naturally comfortable. I worked together with my husband Gero Grundmann and we found that our initial uneasiness with the maggots had vanished very quickly. We found that changing mindsets through the design process was the important thing and that we

could probably change the image others have of maggots as well, so we decided to design experiences that would enable us to achieve this. The questionnaires that gave the creatures names, identities, professions, likes and dislikes, and dreams of the future proved very effective. At our intervention at Tate Modern people at first didn't want to step closer to the table where we posed the questions. They were shocked, of course, but that was just an indication of the point from which we were pushing their boundaries. But once the audience's attention was engaged they even named the maggots and showed real concern for the fate of individual creatures after the event, saying, for example, 'What happens to Tom now? You're not going to kill him, are you?' Something had clearly changed.

Different value systems apply to the same object. I see materials, animals and objects based on their value of being, rather than monetary value. I use objects where I find a discrepancy between these two value systems. I try to transform materials that are undervalued by the market into objects that reflect their inherent value in a way that other people can see.

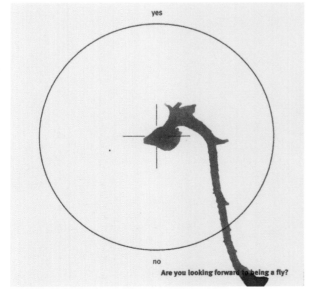

yes

no

Are you looking forward to being a fly?

70. (*opposite*)
Maggotypes, 2001

71. (*above*)
Lasting Void stool, 2007

72. (*right*)
Lasting Void, production process,
2007

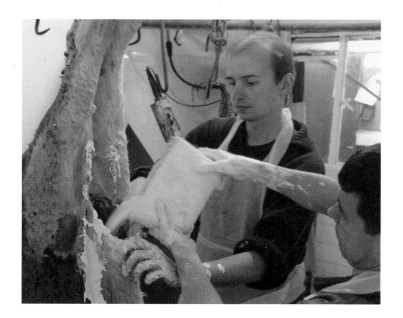

To reassign value it is sometimes necessary to relieve the object from the context and value system with which it is currently associated. The 'Ruminant Bloom' lamps (fig.68) are a good example. To re-contextualize the stomach it was necessary to distance it from the social norms that weigh it down, so I removed it from the context of potential food.

Gareth Williams: Latterly your work has turned away from animals towards an exploration of the potential of the vegetable world to supply new resources. You undertake this in an experimental and artistic fashion, for example by setting up workshops to discover the properties of seaweed, and by creating series of forms that are, to a greater or lesser degree, functional. Do you intend this work to remain as art, or as low-level craft production, or are these tentative steps towards industrial production? I'm interested to hear you talk about industry and mass production, since so much of your work has consciously taken place outside that sphere. Is this because you are not interested in the mass market, or large-scale production? Is there an ethical or other reason why you don't engage with this system?

Julia Lohmann: On a practical level, it requires a huge investment from companies to start developing a new material or design process, which may have potential, but which is also full of potential risks. Working with galleries allows me to develop materials in a more fluid way, without having to convince a hierarchical organization lacking design thinking at the top that it might be worth doing. Industrial producers need to see the case-study designs I produce to accept that a material like seaweed is a viable raw material. Once again, I use objects to communicate ideas and potential where language, or in this case figures, would fall short. I don't see the gallery and industrial fields as separate, but instead as different parts of the same process, the former a potential staging post for the latter. For me, design galleries are a place for research and development.

Working with galleries enables you to think freely, with quite an open brief, instead of developing work while constantly considering commercial parameters. If you start with an open mind you can develop opportunities you would have to steer clear of in industrial design processes. You can make more of exploration, investigating incongruities and other anomalies that are normally eliminated. If you edit ideas quickly, you might be reducing research cost and time, but you also develop fewer ideas, limiting your creative potential.

73.
Kelp Constructs installation, 2008
Galeria Nilufar, Milan

74.
Laminarium installation,
2010
Stanley Picker Gallery,
Kingston University

17

Glithero

'We're always trying to capture this moment when something becomes what it is from nothingness, so we're trying to create that moment in the purest gesture.'

Conventionally, the modernist industrial definition of design matched function to requirement: a well-designed product efficiently answered the needs of its user. Based on this principle, mass production and accelerated consumption have conspicuously succeeded, leaving space for some designers to step back from the imperative of defining their design practice in these terms. Instead, they explore the outer margins of making and using objects, often by assuming the stance of latter-day craftspeople analysing materials and techniques. In itself this is not a new response to industrial production; the Arts and Crafts movement thrived over a century ago. What is new today is the element of performance that designers add to their work. Not content with merely creating pieces that stand outside the conventions of industrial design, they now wish to include their own participation as integral to the result.

This is true of Glithero, an Anglo-Dutch partnership that seeks to capture and present the actual moment they make an object, often in the inherent character of the objects, but also in sophisticated films recording their production. British born Tim Simpson (born 1982) met Sarah van Gameren (born 1981) from the Netherlands at the Royal College of Art, and both graduated in 2006. In 2008 they formed Glithero to pursue a common interest in 'time-based installations'. Their work encompasses furniture, objects and installations, as well as film-making and books. They chose the name Glithero for the studio because it is the maiden name of Simpson's mother and also because it sounds a little like the Dutch word for 'glitter', so it had resonance for them both.

Very early in their careers, Simpson and van Gameren composed a manifesto that continues to shape and inform their production:

> The machine will perform
> The machine will create a product
> The process is more important than the product
> The work will have an audience
> The work will be accessible to all
> The work will be understood by children[1]

In broad terms their materials define their output. Early projects explored how wax acts when it is molten. The designers created a candle-making machine, an elaborate construction of motorized arms and wires lowering wicks into vats of heated wax. The machine has taken different forms, variously making individual candles ('Panta Rei', 2008) and multi-headed wax chandeliers ('Big Dipper', 2007, figs 77 and 78) which, in the case of the 'Big Black Beast' (2008), require a tonne-vat of molten wax, incorporate 32 candles and can be a metre in diameter. The complex mechanism allows the layering of wax around the wick to be experienced as a performance and the artefacts that are produced are testament to the process of their own production.

Wax is momentarily fluid but sets hard, also a characteristic of plaster and Jesmonite, a gypsum-based material in an acrylic resin. 'Running Mould' (2010, fig. 75) was a project at Z33 Gallery in Hasselt, Belgium, where the two designers poured wet plaster directly on to the gallery floor. As each layer was about to cure, they ran a profiled mould along it, repeating the process many times to create a curved 12-metre-long bench where, in their own words, 'the duality of product and process strive to be one and the same'.[2] The bench appropriates the traditional technique of moulding cornices, but on a massive scale, requiring three and a half tonnes of plaster and a team of nine to make it. It also reminds us of Anish Kapoor's sculpture 'Svayambh' (2009; deriving from the Sanskrit word meaning 'self-generated'), a monumental wax slab shaped by the architrave of a door as it mechanically enters and exits the gallery in which it is installed. The notion of the self-generated object is explored here too, and in 'The Long Drop' (fig. 79), an installation created by Glithero for the exhibition *Lapse in Time*, curated by Hans Maier-Aichen during the Experimenta festival in Lisbon, September 2009.

Even more than 'Running Mould', this work was a performance spectacle. The designers built a 12-metre-long twisting timber mould like a rollercoaster, down which they poured successive waves of liquid Jesmonite. Like lava from a volcano, the material found its own level and final resting place depending on its setting point. Once the mould

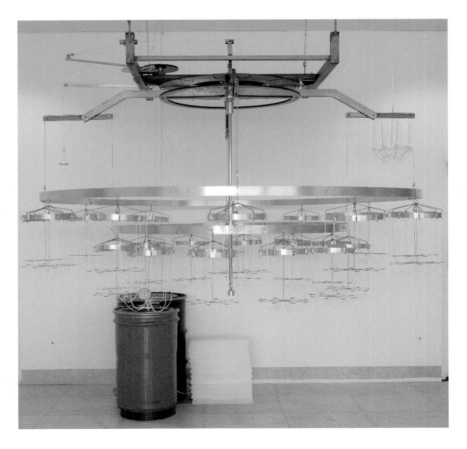

was filled, it was removed, leaving a table connected to a winding feeding chute, expressive of the way in which it had been fabricated. As Tim Simpson has said, 'We're always trying to capture this moment when something becomes what it is from nothingness, so we're trying to create that moment in the purest gesture'. Possibly in part due to the sculptural materials of these projects, in many ways Simpson and van Gameren seem to be talking and acting like sculptors rather than industrial designers, for example: 'The twelve-metre-long table disregards the idea of design being determined by cost or transport efficiency. Our aim is juxtaposition.' Furthermore they describe 'The Long Drop' not as furniture but as a 'space-filling, site-specific installation'.[3]

Other projects are more closely aligned with conventions of design and industrial production, such as 'Blueware' (fig.76), a series of experiments marrying light-sensitive dyes and ceramics, first seen when Glithero participated in the Fendi-sponsored *Craft Punk* exhibition during the Milan furniture fair in 2009. The technique involves creating photograms (camera-less photographs) by laying objects directly on to surfaces coated with light-sensitive chemicals. Early photograms in the nineteenth century were often botanical illustrations, and Glithero has created its own series of 'Blueware' vases and tiles recording the flora of Camden's streets around its London studio. The strident blue tone recalls blueprints, the now-obsolete technique of reproducing large-format designs such as architectural plans. Both photograms and blueprints are redundant technologies, revived and reinvigorated by the designers who place them in new contexts, rather as Troika and rAndom International approach the digital technologies of the recent past.

The last material with which Simpson and van Gameren have experimented is paper. In 2008 they exhibited 'Les French', a collection of furniture, at Gallery Fumi in London. The frames were initially made of bamboo canes tied simply together with string. To give them stability, these were cast in bronze using the lost-material technique. In contrast to the now heavy and stable bases the designers improvised containers into the frames by wrapping areas with gummed paper tape. The contrasting values of bronze and paper are at the heart of the piece.

Glithero contributed a project about paper to an exhibition exploring the nature of handmade objects staged by *Wallpaper** magazine during the Milan furniture fair in 2011. Working closely with specialist print firm Baddeley Brothers, the studio designed five paper planes that celebrated the company's printing abilities and appropriated the function of an envelope-making machine (fig.80). The planes were shown alongside the studio's film that recorded the project and the relationship of the printers to their machines. The purpose and function of this project, if it must have one, is to act as communication. Throughout their practice Glithero combine making, performance, communicati and spectacle. Sometimes their work is an adjunct of public relations as with the projects for Fendi and *Wallpaper**, at other times it belon metaphorically and literally in the gallery space. It all derives from t discourse of design, craft-making and industrial production, and as su demonstrates the broad spectrum of practice possible in design toda

79.
The Long Drop
installation, 2009
Experimenta, Lisbon

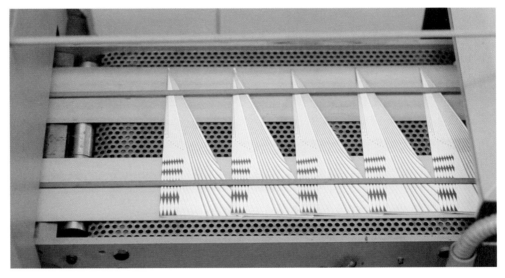

18

Fredrikson Stallard

'We have a constant love affair with the freedom of the fine art world, but as we always tend to pull this inspiration into functional objects, we must, at the end of the day, call ourselves designers.'

Like many European designers in this book, Swedish-born Patrik Fredrikson (born 1968, *opposite, left*) came to Britain as a student, and stayed. He arrived in 1995 to study industrial design at Central St Martin's where he met Essex-born Ian Stallard (born 1973, *right*), and the pair eventually founded their studio in 2002. The expansion of a collector's market for high-end design aligned with the art market in the first decade of this century required the invention of new kinds of designers attuned to debates in art and capable of producing highly distinctive signature works. Taking their inspiration from diverse sources such as pop art, deconstructivist architecture and the materials in which they work, Fredrikson and Stallard have developed a body of work that has mostly resided in the luxury, gallery and limited-edition markets, with clients that include Swarovski, Chanel, Bernhardt Design, David Gill Galleries, The London Design Festival, Veuve Clicquot and the Savoy Hotel.

Gareth Williams: We encounter your work most frequently in the context of prestigious gallery exhibitions, exclusive private commissions, or in high-profile corporate commissions where design can be said to be an adjunct of public relations. Is it fair to say that you see your work in terms of 'premium design', and as part of a luxurious and elite context? Is this intentional, and have you consciously steered your career in this direction? Or is it simply that you make the work you want to make and this is where it lives?

Fredrikson Stallard: We never set out to live primarily in the gallery world at all, in fact we set out to work the other way around, but the world wasn't ready for our visual language in industrial mass-produced products and furniture. We always try to push, not only ourselves, but also the concept of design. Often our work takes on an aesthetic or manufacturing process that isn't suitable for the mass market. But (as the saying goes) what is avant-garde today is mainstream tomorrow. Over the last few years we have started to work with mass producers that share our vision. We always set out to work on many levels. It is difficult, as people desperately want to put you in certain pre-labelled boxes, which we always strongly resist.

Gareth Williams: Does your work principally derive from concepts or the exploration of materials? You seem to take different approaches for different projects. For example, the 'King Bonk' chair (2008, fig.81) arose from experiments with form-making by distorting materials, to create entirely original furniture shapes. The 'Pyrenees' sofa (2007) came about by a similar process. On the other hand, the 'Gasoline Garden' vases (2009, fig.82) are all about 'the concept'. You chose forms and materials with specific historical and cultural connotations, and the success of the vases in part relies on our ability to read those references. You didn't touch the vases at all in the course of their fabrication, but you crafted the original prototypes for 'King Bonk' yourselves. On one hand you think through making, on the other you design the object to accord to your concept. Can you talk about the relationship of hand and eye, craftsmanship and conceptualization, in your work?

Fredrikson Stallard: There is always a relationship between hand, eye, craftsmanship and concept. The concept always comes first, because without a concept or reference we simply can't operate. In some of our work, such as the 'Gasoline Garden' vases, the concept sits on several levels and in these circumstances it is inevitable, and unavoidable, that one level will take on a more dominant role.

Our work is always layered, and sometimes one layer shines through more than another, this doesn't necessarily have to mean these pieces come from different approaches. With the 'Gasoline Garden' vases you are correct to the point that the concept may have taken on more of a physical presence, rather than lying more submissively behind the expression of the materials.

We always try to be as physically involved as possible in a body of work, but this isn't imperative. With most pieces we make the first initial model, 'the mother form' or blueprint,

ourselves. This was the case with 'King Bonk' and 'Pyrenees', as well as with the 'Gasoline Garden' vases. We have a hands-on approach to most of our work and like to think we know our crafts, but since we refuse to lock ourselves in with a certain process or material it would prove impossible to surround ourselves with every tool, machine, or high craft skill to make our work a reality. If we have an idea, we work on finding a way to do it. Therefore we have to work with people outside our studio. We are rigorous in choosing these people and develop a very close working relationship with them, but sometimes we have to physically work on pieces ourselves if this is best for what we want to achieve.

As an example, when working on the 'Gasoline Garden' vases, we made all the original forms of the vases, we photographed the women in their positions, 'styled' their expressions and postures how we wanted them to be, and retouched the photographs, moving arms and legs, collaging them to fit perfectly on to the final vase forms. Some of these steps called for professionals to aid with technical aspects, to achieve the result we wanted. We were essentially painting on a three-dimensional canvas. The surface imagery itself was applied under our strict supervision by a carefully selected airbrush artist. We chose from six different painters, who each did a test vase with the same imagery, and we picked the one we felt understood our vision the best. The imagery with the women, flames and smoke is a carefully orchestrated surface design that we created with technical help from some great craftspeople and technicians.

We intended the pieces to be contemporary versions of Ming vases so it was important to us that they were made in the same way and even in the same place as the originals. In some ways the use of materials was more experimental than with 'King Bonk' and 'Pyrenees', as we were using car paints and lacquers on porcelain rather than traditional glaze. This combination of extremely

81. (*page 159, previously*)
King Bonk chair, 2008

82. (*above*)
Gasoline Garden vases, 20

opposed craft techniques is contextually challenging as well as being the best manufacturing technique to achieve the detailed painterly finish the pieces needed to have.

All our finished pieces are carefully controlled and made with great precision. When does a piece stop being experimental, and what is the next step? In our view, experiments more often than not go wrong, and for us they are things that stay in the studio and are used to develop new pieces rather than being themselves something to be published. But maybe it could be a very interesting exhibition to allow these to come out of the box and take centre stage one day?

With the 'King Bonk' chair and 'Pyrenees' sofa, the original pieces are in a sense sculptures by the artists, working with materials in an unorthodox way, allowing them to express themselves by twisting and carving highly evocative forms, that may seem superficially (aesthetically) pleasing, but to us their true life beats underneath as a passport for new ways of allowing materials to exist. An honest approach we guess.

Essentially what interests us is the psychological relationship between the object and the observer. Our work sits on a platform of technology, craft and concept, allowing the work to undergo some kind of metamorphosis in the process from concept to final piece. Technology plays a huge role and we often encourage new technology to seep into older conceived ideas to create new solutions. 'King Bonk' derived from expressing a particular material's key characteristics, in this case polyurethane foam and its elasticity and softness. We were allowing this material, originally developed for its completely utilitarian qualities, to be expressive. This quest to set materials 'free', to revise their use, to let a material evolve without actually changing any of its original properties is fascinating, and to allow the end product to communicate this to the user, to allow the 'consumer' (if you like) to connect with this

material in a new way, is rewarding. We introduce new qualities; they may be aesthetic or utilitarian.

Gareth Williams: 'Portrait' (a sculpture sponsored by Veuve Clicquot for the London Design Festival, 2008, fig. 83) was an interesting project to me, because you engaged with scale and materiality in a new way, and stepped further away from issues of function than usual. 'Portrait' is a work of design in the sense that you designed and specified an outcome that would suit a client, a time, a place and a sponsor. But these 'functions' are not conventional industrial design outcomes: 'Portrait' didn't 'do' anything, it simply 'was'. I suppose my question here is, did this project feel different than, say, designing a large chandelier like 'Pandora' (2007, fig. 60, for Swarovski), which has similar purposes of impact and image-making though with a greater sense of functionality and utility? Or do you regard 'Portrait' as 'sculpture' in the terms a fine artist might think about their work? Does 'Portrait' mean something? Is it possible to 'design' an 'artwork'?

Fredrikson Stallard: I think it is fair to say the functions of 'Portrait' are maybe not what one might imagine as conventional industrial design outcomes, but we are not conventional industrial designers either. This is increasingly the kind of brief designers like us are receiving and making a living from, rather than 'design a comfortable orthopaedic office chair' etc. We live in a new world and established typologies such as 'form follows function' have started to cease, and to expand our vision we need to write and create new typologies for ourselves to survive and to give new platforms for the generations to come. This is one of the most fascinating aspects of our profession.

Both 'Portrait' and 'Pandora' were designed to a brief, where the brief deliberately set out to push us towards the crossover areas of art and design. We were asked to 're-interpret the chandelier' or 'create a beacon for the London

Design Festival'. Both, with their sites and installation parameters encourage spectacle and unconventionality. Both Swarovski's Crystal Palace collection and Veuve Clicquot's site-specific pieces are platforms where the creator doesn't have to feel they are being forced to do either art or design. These clients, or patrons, give design a tremendous amount of creative freedom and it would be up to the creator, the designer, the artist, to choose the path and set the scene. The 'function' for both pieces was to create a sensorial impact, which is essentially an objective of fine art.

'Pandora' doesn't have a greater sense of functionality or utility than 'Portrait', in fact one could argue the other way around. 'Portrait' could act as a light, or as an architectural element in a building or landscape. 'Pandora' did not actually contain any lights at all, and in that sense was perhaps even less of a utilitarian object.

Another thought is how 'selfishly' you are thinking as a designer. We do have to concern ourselves with some sort of end user, whatever we create or design. In the high-end gallery world it would be the collector, and the more sophisticated clientele that would appreciate and maybe be prepared to eschew some level of comfort/function in exchange for a little more context/emotion. Would there be a point in designing a 10-metre-long sofa that only can seat three people and not very comfortably? We would argue yes, there would be a point in doing this, as long as you know your motives and keep to these, and the purpose of this would probably not to be part of a domestic or commercial environment, but to sit as a commentary on our contemporary lives.

We have a constant love affair with the freedom of the fine art world, but as we always tend to pull this inspiration into functional objects, we must, at the end of the day, call ourselves designers.

83. (*opposite*)
Portrait installation, 2008
Somerset House, London

Martino Gamper

'I'm a designer in that my work is functional and I care about the usability of my products but an artist in that I like to think about what my work means in its particular context.'

In the decade or so since Martino Gamper (born 1971) graduated from the RCA he has earned a reputation as an easy-going designer of sociable spaces and events, a popular figure at the centre of a network of collaborative exhibitions, projects and 'happenings' on the London design scene. Emily King has curated Martino's work in several exhibitions and calls his furniture 'agents of easy sociability', emphasizing how Gamper's design philosophy is about bringing people and things together.[1] She expands her point: 'Martino doesn't just make lovely objects, he creates happy spaces, I know that sounds sappy, but it's true.'[2] His bonhomie is natural but his modesty conceals great determination and self-belief, demonstrated by self-publishing his work in a series of books with titles like *What Martino Gamper did between two-thousand and two-thousand&four*. His signature approach to furniture design has been to assemble one-off pieces from the salvaged remains of mass-produced items, seemingly wedding craftsmanship and technology while not incidentally creating highly visible, even 'sculptural' and collectible unique pieces. At first 'making do and mending' on London's cultural eastern fringe, by 2008 Martino was a feted international designer, a star of the emerging 'design art' scene.

Raised in Merano in northern Italy near the Austrian border, Gamper trained in cabinetmaking and then moved to Vienna, where he initially studied sculpture under Michelangelo Pistoletto before switching to industrial design with Matteo Thun. He was among the first cohort to be recruited in 1998 for the newly formed Design Products MA at the Royal College of Art by Ron Arad, himself a designer often working

at the boundaries with art. Gamper dislikes defining himself but his grounding in craft, design and art is evident: 'I'm a designer in that my work is functional and I care about the usability of my products but an artist in that I like to think about what my work means in its particular context. And I create like a craftsman, using traditional tools to make things out of other things.'[3]

Several themes have emerged and persisted in his work, the first being an interest in designing furniture for the corners of rooms, or which use corners in their construction. Gamper has explained his motivation, which was as much artistic and conceptual as it was about solving functional issues. 'In that respect I think I've always worked more like an artist. Rather than being interested in designing a new chair or table I've always followed a kind of upper-concept for my furniture. In the instance with the corner I was interested in exploring a physical space that informs furniture … Corners are somehow the starting point of any space, the x, y and z that form a tri-dimensional space interested me as a starting point to think about furniture and interiors.'[4] Corners can offer a sense of security and privacy, but can also be claustrophobic and stuffy. Emily King has written: 'conventional interior designers are afraid of corners. They draw furniture away from the extremes of the room and cluster it, like guests at a cocktail party, at its centre. By pushing back toward the room's edges, Martino seeks out social interaction that is less polite, but more compelling.'[5] This may be rather overstating it, but Gamper's interest resulted in several eye-catching sofas, benches and shelves, most notably in his RCA degree show in 2000 and for a British Council exhibition about new British independent publishing called *The Book Corner*, first shown in Milan in 2002.

A second theme has been more enduring and has been largely responsible for the critical success Gamper now enjoys. He creates assemblages of discarded or deconstructed furniture components to make new items, in a process akin to collage or musical sampling. On one hand it is like sketching in three dimensions to find new furniture forms, but crucially, on the other hand assemblage relieves Gamper from the responsibility of designing anything original himself. Collaborating with the furniture-maker Rainer Spehl, Gamper presented 'Furniture While U Wait' at the annual V&A Village Fete in the summer of 2001 and again in 2002, making furniture from discarded materials and salvaged parts to create bespoke new items. As much performance as it was furniture design, the spontaneity of the process was its essence. The approach led to a collection of one-off pieces, again with Spehl, called 'We Make Remake', and ultimately to Gamper's best-known project, '100 Chairs in 100 Days', completed in 2007 (fig. 84). The 100 chairs he made can be seen as a series of quotes from high and low design history, a chatter of design

35. (*opposite*)
Two Legged console from
the series Gio Ponti translated
by Martino Gamper, 2007, with
production process of If Gio
Only Knew furniture, 2007
Design Miami/Basel
Galeria Nilufar, Milan

ideas interacting with one another. They are all unique, but since they are literally made from old furniture, they cannot be seen as entirely original designs.

Gamper has explained that his project was in part a commentary on the impossible constraint of designing the 'perfect' high-volume mass-produced chair. 'That's something that interests me: can you do mass production but also make each chair different – mass-produced individuality?'[6] He also enjoyed the anthropological perspective that his creations gave new life to discarded furniture with their own histories of use. High in concept, therefore, the project also displayed Gamper's considerable craftsmanship and ingenuity in creating furniture that could still be used. It was an artistic approach to a design issue, a position that Gamper willingly occupies. 'The project doesn't make sense in any respect – financially, creatively or in terms of practicality – but this was what attracted me to the idea. It was my own response to normal, expected systems of manufacturing that dominate design. Creating 100 different chairs, one a day, was a process of sorts but each chair has its own character. It was a form of manufacturing that actively defies the uniformity that people expect from manufactured products.'[7]

Gamper clearly enjoyed the process of making this series of chairs, which he regarded as, in some sense, research towards an idealized mass-produced chair. The writer Alexandros Stavrakos took another point of view with which I have sympathy. 'This resuscitation that you attempt can, actually be seen as very melancholic. Mutilated parts glued together may have taken up a new shape, but they are clearly odd, displaced, even monstrous, not in an aesthetic way but in a symbolic way.'[8] Certainly many of the chairs are awkward and offer little or no design improvement on the original chairs that sired them. Should we, therefore, regard them as ironic references or postmodern jokes? Gamper admits some chairs in the series are ugly but finds a rationale to qualify them. 'I'm challenging my taste, and some of it might be on the edge of being very ugly, but that's always been one of my concerns: where does ugliness begin and where does beauty start?'[9]

In early 2007 Ron Arad introduced Martino Gamper to Nina Yashar, proprietor of the Milanese design gallery Nilufar, who has subsequently presented his one-off furniture. Gamper discovered that his gallerist owned furniture designed by Gio Ponti for the Hotel Parco dei Principo, Sorrento, in 1961, and proposed a project called 'If Gio Only Knew', to be shown at the Design Miami/Basel fair in Basel in June 2007 (fig. 85). Gamper deconstructed Ponti's highly collectible original furniture and from the parts he built his own works, all as a live performance on the opening night of the fair. Once again, the constraint of working in a

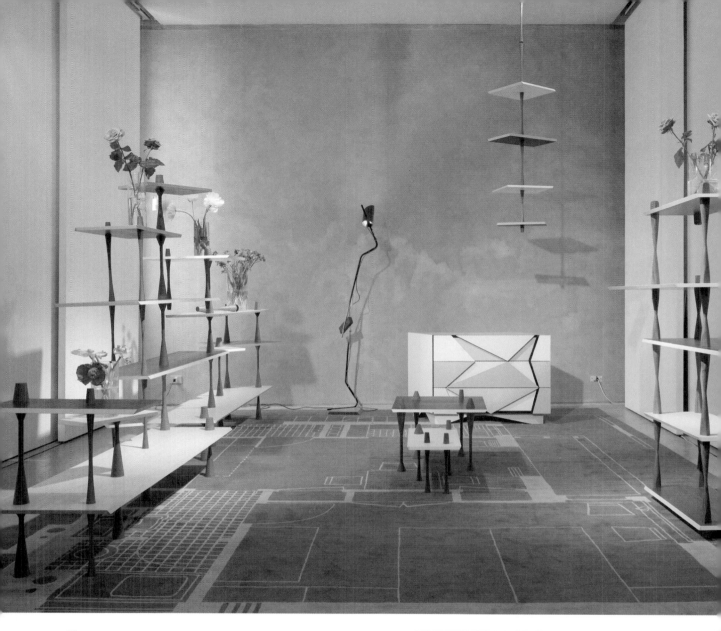

86.
Composizioni furniture, 2011
Galeria Nilufar, Milan

short time frame gave Gamper a sense of spontaneity. 'The idea of creating something new without a particular drawing and concept, in front of an audience, creates a certain pressure that pushes me towards work that is less conceptual and controlled and more driven by intuition and emotion.'[10] Was this vandalism or an act of homage to Ponti? His performance drew criticism from more conservative design collectors but sealed his position as a prominent design practitioner. The following year he was named a Designer of the Future by Design Miami/Basel, along with Max Lamb, Julia Lohmann and Kram/Weisshaar.

Gamper's sociability underlies his design practice and the two come together with an ongoing series of pop-up trattoria events he organizes with various collaborators. Designing and cooking are similar activities to Gamper: they both involve the creative reinterpretation of ingredients and principles in a given time and place, and the results are enjoyed through the senses. The food, the furniture and the decorations are all created specially for the events that have taken place in bars and galleries. 'This is part of my life, not just a design project but a gathering of friends … it's about not dividing your life and your practice.'[11]

Until recently Gamper has been content at design's edges, producing his quirky one-off assemblages for the gallery sector. 'The idea of multiplication didn't really appeal', he said in an interview in 2008. 'I never got a kick out of seeing fifty of the same chair. I'm more interested in the individual.'[12] But latterly he has made his first foray towards the elusive goal of the perfect mass-produced chair, with the 'Vigna' chair for Magis, first shown in 2010. Part bistro chair, part retro design, the wire and plastic construction recalls bentwood Thonet chairs and garden furniture while not being slavish to either. The formal experiments of his '100 Chairs…' project evidently helped him to refine the proportions and materials for his first design for mass production.

Gamper's work is now much sought-after. He has contributed to British Council exhibitions in China, his '100 Chairs…' project was shown in California, and he continues to exhibit with Nilufar in Milan (fig.86). *Wallpaper** magazine pronounced him 'Best Alchemist' in 2008 and commissioned him to build a triumphal arch of chairs in the John Madejski Garden at the V&A for the London Design Festival in 2009. London remains his home. 'It creates opportunities for everyone in terms of work, exchanging ideas and sharing experiences,' he says. 'There's a sense of freedom. People don't judge you and you can get on with what's important.'[13]

20

Paul Cocksedge

'I like to surprise people. I like to challenge people. I like to have fun, you know?'

Paul Cocksedge (born 1978) brings an alchemic sense of wonder to contemporary British design. His work, mostly broadly in the realm of lighting, encompasses one-off experimental installations and special commissions, as well as an increasing number of products intended for mass production. What they have in common is a wow factor usually derived from the audience's questioning of how something is made to work. He is a latter-day wizard, using high and low technology to create modern marvels.

Ron Arad, his former professor at the Royal College of Art, has said that as a student Paul was 'unprofessional and slightly childish and helpless. But this innocent, child-like thing is part of the way he operates.... He's still very cocky but his helplessness is one of the best weapons in his arsenal.'[1] Cocksedge's cheekiness may have directly influenced Arad's decision to accept his application to the Design Products MA course in 2000: he filled his portfolio with counterfeit £10 notes. Cocksedge recalls, 'It was just a way of getting noticed, but I think I've kept that cheekiness in the work I do. I like to surprise people. I like to challenge people. I like to have fun, you know?'[2] Once at the RCA, Cocksedge thrived in the climate of freedom he encountered and has subsequently striven to maintain that sense of freedom in his projects. Ron Arad created the model for contemporary industrial designers to think of themselves as autonomous self-initiators and has said, 'Paul is one of the best examples we've had of someone who was plucked from the anonymous world of industrial design into being the author of his own work'.

Presented with a student brief to grow an object, Cocksedge observed what happened to humble polystyrene cups when they were heated in an oven. As they melted, 'to me they seemed to come alive as though they were dancing and transformed from disposable mass-produced products to precious unique forms'.[3] Immediately after his graduation

in 2002 he made one-off 'Styrene' lampshades (fig. 88) by melting shrunken and distorted cups together into spheres. At the same time he founded his own studio with Joana Pinho, his business partner whom he met at the RCA. Pinho manages business and strategy for the studio leaving Cocksedge free to take the creative lead.

Cocksedge's natural inquisitiveness is, perhaps, a child-like trait, as is his willingness to dream. 'I sometimes like to let my mind go to make-believe land,' he says, 'because it's a really interesting way to find inspiration, to find a beginning or to search for a shape, or find ways of people interacting. You separate yourself from the day-to-day. If you start to daydream, sometimes something quite interesting happens.'[4] This is why some of his projects may seem so improbable, but they are also often arresting and poetic. 'Life 01' (fig. 87) is a lamp developed for the Italian manufacturer Flos in 2009 that started as a project some years earlier, in 2003. It takes the form of a simple crystal flower vase. When a flower stem is introduced it acts as an electrical conductor through the water, causing the vase to illuminate from below for the duration of the flower's life. As the flower withers, its conductivity reduces and the lamp slowly dims. The designer compares it to a memento mori, an allegory of the transience of life. It is far from practical but neither is it intended to be a task-light, so utility is only a small part of its function.

'NeON' (fig. 90) also originated in the highly productive period around the time of Cocksedge's graduation from the RCA. It comprises hand-made glass containers filled with neon gas that, in daylight, are transparent but in darkness glow vividly. The designer enjoyed personalizing an established industrially manufactured lighting source, and highlighting the magical way an invisible gas becomes visible when an electric current runs through it. Once again, the lamp is near useless as a conventional product, but is a highly evocative visual demonstration of ubiquitous processes that are normally concealed. It won Cocksedge the Bombay Sapphire prize in 2003, an award for innovative use of glass. In 2007 Cocksedge returned to neon lighting to create an enormous installation for the Wellcome Trust in central London, a wealthy medical charity that has also been a patron of Doshi Levien and Julia Lohmann. His installation was a photograph of two outspread arms, each 11 metres long, stretching across the building's windows. The photograph was printed on to conductive film that is opaque when a current runs through it, but transparent when neutral, revealing the veins and arteries illustrated anatomically correctly in neon tubes. Paul Cocksedge wanted the effect to be like peeling away the skin to reveal the body's workings within and intended it as a metaphor for the Wellcome Trust's activities.

89. (*above*)
Veil installation, 2008
Swarovski Crystal
Palace collection

90. (*right*)
NeON lights, 2003

With little interest in designing mass-produced products, Cocksedge rapidly gained a reputation for his highly personal, quirky installations that always seemed to ask the question 'what if?' His dramatic and often surprising design statements were perfect for a decade in which corporate patrons embraced design innovation. Cocksedge produced several projects for the Swarovski Crystal Palace collection, but all remain one-off pieces. He directed lasers at individual crystals that refracted light beams to form the outline of a large crystal in space to make 'Crystallize' (2004). For 'Veil' (2008, fig.89) Cocksedge created a curtain of 1,440 interconnected crystals. Magically, when viewed in a mirror, the features of the Mona Lisa appeared across the piece, but were invisible when it was viewed directly. Cocksedge, who is normally happy to describe his alchemical processes, preferred to keep his own counsel about how he achieved the effect, but it is likely to result from subtle angling of certain crystals within the grid, that could only be detected from the fixed point of the mirror.

Cocksedge has designed other magical installations, for example 'Kiss', a project presented first in Milan then London in 2009. Inspired by the tradition of kissing beneath the mistletoe at Christmas, Cocksedge created LED installations (in Milan it was in the ceiling of the imposing Galleria Vittorio Emanuele II, and in London's Covent Garden it was in a Christmas tree). The lights were activated by kissing couples, whose embrace completed the electrical circuit. The installations were the fruition of a much earlier idea in which a drawing in graphite acted as a light switch: by adding the final line connecting the others, the wielder of the pencil could switch on a light. As with 'Veil', the interaction of the audience with 'Kiss' was integral, becoming in this instance an essential component of the mechanism. 'Kiss' was more than just a spectacle; it aimed to raise money for charity (the kisses were sponsored by a bank).

As Cocksedge has brought people closer into his projects, social considerations have increasingly arisen. For the London Design Festival in 2010, Cocksedge designed 'Drop' for a prominent site on the terrace outside the Royal Festival Hall. 'Drop' looked just like a huge bent copper penny that had fallen from the sky, now resting on one edge. In fact it was magnetically charged so it could attract coins, which would leap from the hands of passers-by. Each penny that was added to 'Drop' was translated into a pound given to the Barnado's children's charity, transforming it into a highly original charity box. The project required intensive engineering and construction, but Cocksedge says: 'I like to dream about the impossible and challenge the engineers I work with.'[5] Here, he was referring specifically to a project intended for the Design Museum's *Super Contemporary* exhibition, called 'Rain It In', in which he wanted to use static generators to deflect the flow of water. He would like to install it across London's Millennium Bridge to deflect the rain away from pedestrians, a project that is as yet unrealized.

Latterly Cocksedge has taken more interest in design for manufacture, working with both Established & Sons and the leading Italian company Flos on lighting projects including 'Skin', a pendant light that exploits the tiny size of LED lights and which appears to be a thin sheet of metal, torn open at one corner to reveal a light source within (shown in the photograph on page 173). It is pleasing that his original thinking finds its way from one-off commissions into the commercial market, because he is essentially an industrial designer (before the RCA he studied Industrial Design at Sheffield Hallam University). And it would be a mistake to write him off as only a designer of quirky lamps and lighting installations. His best work, such as 'Life 01', and a recent installation at the Victoria and Albert Museum called 'A Gust of Wind' (2010, fig. 91), are poetic and artistic descriptions of life's fragility, and are surprisingly sensitive coming from a designer known for his cheeky insouciance. 'A Gust of Wind' comprises 300 folded pieces of Corian, a synthetic ceramic, suspended to appear like sheets of paper blowing in the wind. Perhaps typically, Cocksedge played down its impact, saying: 'It isn't complicated. It's just a light, positive, very dreamy piece.'[6]

21

Committee

'Artworks specifically about design practice'

Harry Richardson and Clare Page (partners in life and work, both born in 1975) are artists who have chosen to be designers. Their trajectory is therefore the opposite of many of the designers in this book, who seem to prefer to act like artists. Trained as painters at Liverpool Art School, from which they graduated in 1998, Page and Richardson found their primary interest to be the world of consumer goods and objects, which led them out of what they perceived as an art-world ghetto towards the more quotidian world that design represents. 'We've always felt like outsiders in the design industry, but there's a definite reason that we didn't go into art: that world is isolated, separate and has its own cathedrals. In design, there's more of a crossover and a dialogue with the ordinary world of commodities.'[1] Their ambivalence towards both the design and art worlds extended to the naming of the home and studio in Deptford, south-east London, where they have lived since 1998. Undecided whether they were founding a gallery (for art) or a shop (for design) they merged the two to make Gallop, a multipurpose display/café/studio space they ambiguously call simply a workshop. Committee, the name they gave their practice, came a little later, in 2001.

With a background in art, Committee's interest has tended more towards the cultural, aesthetic and communicative potential of products than to a concern for materials, or the techniques of making. Largely, they have looked at the existing world of goods and what they describe as 'the drama of the everyday' from which to create new works, often travelling no further than the street markets and fly-tipped rubbish of their own neighbourhood for inspiration and source material. 'We have a saying, "Deptford provides", because everything we need we can find here. Deptford is untouched', they have declared.[2] Signature works, such as the 'Kebab' lamp (fig. 92), first shown in 2003, are constructed of found, recycled and salvaged items, mostly kitsch ornaments or decorative components of other products, which they have sourced locally. They skewer these to create unique standard-lamp bases in configurations they believe have their own internal narrative, and which they hope are 'a celebration of the very human instinct to aspire to the absolutes of

92. (*opposite*)
Surprise lamp, 2010, from the
Kebab Lamp series, begun 2003

beauty, elegance and sexiness from the jumble of everyday existence'.[3]
The results are ironic, whimsical, often silly and definitely surreal, but
have proven to be collectible: now they restrict production to eight lamps
per year, traded through Established & Sons.

Giving a new lease of life to discarded and obsolete artefacts is not a
unique approach to design (think of Martino Gamper's '100 Chairs
in 100 Days', for example) but Committee hate to be regarded simply
as designers who recycle, because their interest in their raw material
comes from somewhere other than an industrial designer's concern for
sustainability and ecological imperatives. Rather, Richardson and Page
take a more ambivalent approach: they are not revolted by consumer
culture but are fascinated by mass production and the values that society
places on goods. 'Consumer products are part of the problem, but they
are fascinating things', says Page. 'Humanity has a need for beauty, so
let's look at it.'[4]

Most of Committee's projects have been self initiated, or commissioned
critical or conceptual projects for exhibitions rather than for the
collectors' market, and it is here that I think their impact on British
design is felt best. One such example arose from an invitation by Emily
Campbell at the British Council to contribute to the exhibition *My World,
New Crafts*, staged in Lisbon in 2005, exploring future roles for craft.
They designed 'Flytip' (2005, fig. 93), inspired by a love of antique
panoramic wallpapers. But they were loath to pastiche history and in
any case the woodblock technique used to print those papers would
be prohibitively expensive now. Instead they photographed fly-tipped
rubbish in and around Deptford and worked the images into 13 silk-
screen designs from which Cole & Son printed wallpaper. Committee
describe the composition, including dolls, cigarette packets, motor-oil
containers, circuit boards, traffic bollards and other assorted flotsam
and jetsam, as 'a waltzing whirlwind of waste, suspended before it
either makes its way up to the heavenly rubbish dump in the sky or
comes tumbling down to earth'.[5] Their patternmaking bears comparison
with similar complex assemblages of objects from the material world
composed by their Dutch peers, Studio Job, around the same time.

It seems that Committee are sampling the material world in a way
comparable to how DJs sample existing tracks to create new music,
a position they share with Martino Gamper and, to an extent, Jaime
Hayon who also took part in *My World, New Crafts*. Hayon subsequently
asked Committee to contribute products to Lladro, the Spanish ceramic
figurine manufacturer for whom he had recently become creative director.
They sampled and adapted traditional models from the company's
archive that share a similarly nostalgic, decorative and kitsch sensibility

93. (*above*)
Flytip wallpaper, 2005
Manufactured by
Cole & Son, London

with their use of found objects (fig. 94). Explaining their relationship with Lladro, Committee have said, 'We are both given to flights of fancy and a desire to turn the real into an imaginative, hyper-real vision that allows one to escape the everyday but which we hope might invite the consideration of fundamental truths too.... The defining feature of our approach was playfulness. Figurines are not "useful" design objects in the obvious sense of the word, so it was important to us that they offered something fun and magical to the viewer.'[6]

With several collections Committee have examined our relationship with consumer goods by using found fragments to create new, functionless, sculptural forms that serve as commentaries and observations rather than industrial prototypes. They are what Professor Tony Dunne at the Royal College of Art describes as 'design fictions', speculative suggestions and provocations about the nature of design and its transformative possibilities. The 'Plastic Fandangos' (2008, fig. 96) were five faux products composed of discarded or salvaged plastic parts of real products, reconfigured with new very specific fictional functions. They included a 'Domestic View Finder', composed of a fire-alarm casing, a toy rolling pin, plumbing parts and a doll's-house window (and other bits), that gently rotates to present a constantly changing viewpoint of a room. The collection is nonsensical and Heath Robinson-esque but also imaginative and unconstrained by conventions of design. This is intentional. As Committee have commented: 'Being follies with exceedingly limited practical purpose, the "Fandangos" are essentially artworks, but they are artworks specifically about design practice. However they can also stand firmly in the ornamental category of design, to be enjoyed as simple compositions of colour and shape or even used for the tiny insignificant functions that they do contain.'[7]

The 'Plastic Relics' collection (2009) was an exercise in future archaeology in which the designers imagined post-oil age archaeologists of the twenty-seventh century consigning new values and purposes to the plastic detritus of our own era. Highly designed but ubiquitous components from vacuum cleaners, toy parts and elsewhere were elevated in status to become the lids of boxes that exactly extruded their outlines. The boxes, made in black lacquer in Japan, suggested the long shadow of the plastic products' origins back to the black oil from which they derived. By reversing the values of plastic and lacquer, and presenting the industrially-made elements on bespoke plinths, as art, Committee invited reconsideration of our value systems.

The third such collection was called 'Lost Twin Ornaments' (fig. 95) and was made as part of a project at Metropolitan Works, at the London Metropolitan University, to launch its new digital manufacturing

94. (*opposite*)
Curiosity figurine, 2008
Manufactured by Lladro, Spain

facilities in 2009. Here, Committee paired two different found plastic components and, using CAD, morphed them together to create a new form. It was important to Committee that they lacked anything more than basic computer skills, as their objects demonstrated the potential of computers to generate their own forms and aesthetic. 'In this case the role of designer was diminished to arbiter and selector of a number of examples, rather than the author or sculptor of a form from scratch.'[8]

Aside from a competent but unremarkable upholstered rocking armchair for SCP (anomalous, for Committee, in that it lacks references to other objects), and the 'Bamboo' lamp, a production-model standard lamp for Moooi akin to the 'Kebab' lamp, Committee have not ventured far into actual product design. Instead, they design work that is about design, its value systems, connotations, ephemeral nature and ultimately the sheer diversity of its manifestation. Their anthropological interest in the cultural role of everyday objects, together with their use of rapid prototyping, draw comparisons with the work of Onkar Kular and Noam Toran, and although Committee add irony and humour, Kular and Toran offer a more nuanced and sophisticated reading of objects.

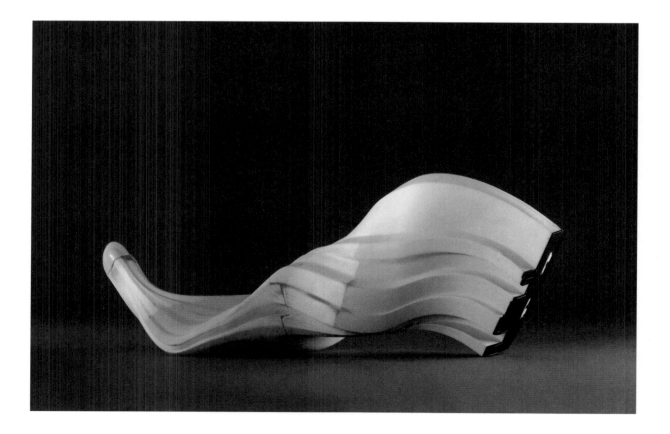

References

21 Twenty One

1 *Industry Insights* report, Design Council, London 2010, p.1.
2 D. Sudjic, *Design in Britain*, London 2009, p.7.
3 *Industry Insights* report, Design Council, London, 2010, p.5, 23 per cent of all UK design businesses are located in London.
4 Ibid., p.9.
5 Ibid., p.2. Figures for 2009:

	Number of Designers	As % of all UK Designers
Freelance designers	65,900	28%
Design consultancies	82,500	36%
In-house teams (100+ people)	83,600	36%

6 Ibid., p.4.
7 'It [the Great Exhibition] also, by extension, acquired for Britain during the period when manufacturing as the essence of economic activity, symbolic "ownership" of the idea of industrial design.' S. Bayley, *Labour Camp: The Failure of Style over Substance*, London 1998, p.58.
8 Sudjic 2009, p.7.
9 Ibid., p.6.
10 M. Leonard, *Britain™: Renewing Our Identity*, London 1997, p.8.
11 Ibid., p.10.
12 Ibid., p.11.
13 Ibid., p.52.
14 Ibid., p.69.
15 Bayley 1998, pp.52, 48.
16 Ibid., p.70.
17 Ibid., p.138.
18 C. Smith, *Creative Britain*, London 1998, p.30.
19 C. Catterall, *Powerhouse::uk*, London 1998, p.5.
20 http://en.wikipedia.org/wiki/Cultural_diplomacy, accessed 17 December 2010.
21 K. Bound et al., *Cultural Diplomacy*, London 2007, pp.11–12.
22 Job advertisement for 'Promoting Britain Worldwide Through Design Officer', April 1996, supplied by Emily Campbell.
23 Emily Campbell, interview with the author, 7 January 2011.
24 E. Campbell, 'Foreword', *Import Export*, British Council, London 2003, p.6.
25 L. Jackson, 'Import Export', *Import Export*, British Council, London 2003, pp. 30–8.
26 http://www.hm-treasury.gov.uk/2011budget_speech.htm.
27 M. Rock, *Mad Dutch Disease / I Heart NL*, lecture given at Premsela, 2004, http://www.2x4.org/_txt/reading_5.html, accessed 8 December 2010.
28 D. West, 'A New Generation', *Icon*, 43, January 2007, p.64.
29 Martino Gamper, quoted in 'Best of 2007', *Financial Times, House & Home*, 12 January 2008 (citing 'Best of 2007 feature, *Wallpaper*', February 2008).
30 Correspondence with the author, 26 May 2011.
31 W. Wiles, 'New Doesn't Always Mean Better', *Icon*, 58, April 2008, p.54.
32 A. Bates, 'Stacks of Talent', *Estd, A Journal from Established & Sons*, 4, Autumn/Winter 2008, p.27.
33 B. Millar, 'The Young Designers Who Like to Play Rough', *The Art Newspaper*, Art Basel Daily edition, 11 June 2009, p.8.
34 D. Charny, 'Federal Animals', in *Under the Same Roof: New designs by the OKAY Studio collective at the Aram Gallery*, London 2008, p.2.
35 Shay Alkalay, quoted in G. Dunmall, 'The Expressionists', *Frame*, 66, January 2009, p.162.

El Ultimo Grito

1 Unattributed article, 'Interview with El Ultimo Grito', no date, www.designboom.com/contemporary/elultimogrito.html, accessed 29 November 2010.
2 L. Jackson, 'Interview with El Ultimo Grito', *Icon*, 17, November 2004, www.iconeye.com, accessed 13 December 2010.
3 W. Wiles and A. Bates, 'Ugly', *Icon*, 61, July 2008, p.53.
4 Regine, 'Interview with El Ultimo Grito', 7 November 2008, www.we-make-money-not-art.com, accessed 29 November 2010.

Raw Edges

1 Yael Mer, quoted in B. Millar, 'The Young Designers Who Like to Play Rough', *The Art Newspaper*, Art Basel Daily edition, 11 June 2009, p.8.
2 Shay Alkalay, quoted in A. Bates, 'Stacks of Talent', *Estd, A Journal from Established & Sons*, 4, Autumn/Winter 2008, p.27.
3 Giulio Cappellini and Yael Mer, quoted in L. Tebbutt, 'A Unique Production', *Grand Designs*, August 2010, pp.47–8.
4 Yael Mer, quoted in O. Stratford, 'The Coiling Collection', *Icon*, 92, February 2011, p.49.
5 Shay Alkalay, quoted in H. Macdonald, 'On the Edge', *Wallpaper*', June 2008, p.90.

Peter Marigold

1 'Back to Basics', interview, *Design 360°*, 25, January 2010, pp.144–9.
2 Peter Marigold, quoted by W. Wiles, *Icon*, 74, August 2009, p.55.
3 P. Green, 'Man Made: Taking Cues from Shop Class, not Art School', *New York Times*, 16 September 2010, pp.1, 8–9.
4 Peter Marigold, quoted by W. Wiles, *Icon*, 52, October 2007, pp.50–1.
5 L. Sellers, *Beau Sauvage*, exhib. cat., Liberty, London 2008.
6 Iterations of this project were shown during the London Design Festival 2010 and again in the exhibition *6 Hands: India Carpenter, Peter Marigold, Ella Robinson*, The Aram Gallery, London, 14 January–19 February 2011.
7 Peter Marigold, quoted in the leaflet accompanying *6 Hands*.
8 Peter Marigold, quoted in 'The Top 50', *Guardian*, 1 September 2007, www.guardian.co.uk/artanddesign/2007/sep/01/design, accessed 21 November 2010.

Max Lamb

1   Le Vin Chin, 'Interview with Max Lamb', 14 July 2008, www.xymara.com, accessed 17 June 2011.
2   Ibid.
3   F. McAuslen, 'London Design Festival People', 17 September 2007, www.timeout.com/london/aroundtown/features/3498/London_Design_Festival_people.html, accessed 10 January 2011.
4   'Max Lamb: Furniture on the Beach', *American Craft Magazine*, December/January 2008, www.americandraftmag.org, accessed 17 June 2011.
5   Le Vin Chin 2011.

Simon Hasan

1   Simon Hasan, quoted in G. Gibson, '"L" for Leather, Simon Hasan', *Crafts*, 214, September/October 2008, p.30.
2   Simon Hasan, quoted in N. Swengley, 'The Trend to Vend', *Evening Standard*, 27 October 2010, www.thisislondon.co.uk/lifestyle/article-23882242-the-trend-to-vend.do, accessed 6 December 2010.
3   Unattributed article, 'Simon Hasan, Product Designer', November 2010, www.stylus.com, accessed at www.simonhasan.com/press on 6 December 2010.
4   Simon Hasan, quoted in F. Rattray, 'Simon Hasan', *i-D Magazine*, 40, January/February 2009, p.86.
5   Simon Hasan, quoted in J. Blackburn, 'Art and Industry', *Financial Times*, 13 February 2010.
6   Unattributed article, 'Simon Hasan, Product Designer', November 2010, www.stylus.com, accessed at www.simonhasan.com/press on 6 December 2010.

Industrial Facility

1   J. Glancey, 'Reductive Power', *Metropolis*, June 2009, www.metropolismag.com, accessed 29 October 2010.
2   Ibid.
3   S. Hecht, 'The Acceleration of Having More with Less', *Ars Electronica*, 2006, www.aec.at, accessed 29 October 2010.
4   Sam Hecht, quoted in 'Milan '09 Preview', *Monitor Unlimited*, 54, Spring 2009. www.monitorunlimited.com, accessed from www.industrialfacility.co.uk, 29 October 2010.
5   S. Hecht, 'Some Recent Acquisitions', *Estd, A Journal from Established & Sons*, 3, 2007, p.29.
6   Ibid.
7   Sam Hecht, quoted in E. Heathcote, 'Discovery of Pleasure in Anonymity', *Financial Times*, 22 February 2007, www.ft.com, accessed 29 October 2010.

Klauser and Carpenter

1   http://matandme.net/klauser-carpenter-moody-open, accessed 24 January 2011.
2   H. Macdonald, 'Very Good & Proper', 4 December 2008, www.wallpaper.com/interiors/very-good-and-proper/2877, accessed 25 January 2011.
3   Ibid.

Doshi Levien

1   K. Bezar, 'Interview with Nipa Doshi', *Dumbo Feather. Pass It On*, 25, Autumn 2010, p.35.
2   Nipa Doshi, quoted in A. Bates, 'Doshi Levien', *Icon*, 55, January 2008, p.62.
3   Nipa Doshi, quoted in G. Gibson, 'A Plural Approach', *Frame*, 58, September/October 2007, p.183.
4   Bezar 2010, p.37.
5   Gibson 2007, p.180.
6   Jonathan Levien, quoted in C. Roux, 'No Rest for the Worldly', *i-D Magazine*, September/October 2007, p.57.
7   Jonathan Levien, quoted in A. Hill, 'Function and Fantasy', *The World of Interiors*, September 2005, p.104.
8   Nipa Doshi, quoted in C. Roux, 'Interview with Doshi Levien', *Swarovski Elements at Work*, 2010, p.8.
9   Gibson 2007, p.183.
10 Bates 2008, p.64.
11 Nipa Doshi, quoted in A. Bates and P. Shaw, 'Milan Furniture Fair 2008>Moroso>Doshi Levien', April 2008, www.iconeye.com, accessed 18 November 2010.
12 Nipa Doshi, quoted in H. Thompson, 'Opposites Attract', *Blueprint*, 212, October 2003, p.90.

Alexander Taylor

1   Correspondence with the author, 10 August 2012.

Jaime Hayon

1   Jaime Hayon, quoted in D. Lutyens, 'The Player', *Observer Magazine*, 10 September 2006, p.41.
2   Jaime Hayon, quoted in P. Davies, 'Think Tank', in *J. Hayon, Backstage*, Barcelona 2006, p.7.
3   Jaime Hayon, quoted in S. Wales, 'He Reigns in Spain', *Vogue Living*, November/December 2006, p.108.
4   Jaime Hayon, quoted in D. Sokol, 'Circus Boy', *Whitewall*, Winter 2006, pp.124–31.
5   K. Long, 'Jaime Hayon', *Icon*, 38, August 2006, p.70.
6   J. Hayon, *Backstage*, Barcelona 2006, p.15.
7   Jaime Hayon, quoted in Sokol 2006.
8   Jaime Hayon, quoted in Davies 2006, p.8.
9   Lutyens 2006, p.40.
10 Jaime Hayon, quoted in E. Schaep, 'Clash and Combine', *Frame*, 49, March/April 2006, p.166.

Troika

1   G. Lucas, 'Troika: Simplicity, playfulness & an essential desire for provocation', *Creative Review*, April 2005, pp.51–2.
2   'Troika', *It's Nice That*, 4, October 2010, p.55.
3   Lucas 2005, p.49.

rAndom International

1   Hannes Koch, quoted in N. Swengley, 'Technology Tamed', *Financial Times*, 12 June 2010, http://www.ft.com/cms/s/2/31fec264-741c-11df-87f5-00144feabdc0.html, accessed 1 November 2010.
2   Hannes Koch, quoted in A. Haden-Guest, untitled essay accompanying the exhibition *The Behaviour of Objects* at Carpenter's Workshop Gallery, London, October 2010.
3   rAndom International, 'Manifesto 28', *Icon*, 50, August 2007, p.84.
4   E. Taub, 'Panels of Light Fascinate Designers', *New York Times*, 6 September 2009, http://www.nytimes.com/2009/09/07/

technology/07bulb.html?_r=2, accessed 15 November 2010.

5   Hannes Koch, quoted in A. Sasaki, 'rAndom International/
    Interview with Hannes Koch', *Hitspaper™*, October
    2009, http://antenna7.com/interview/interview-
    randominternational/index.html, accessed 1 November 2010.

6   Haden-Guest 2010.

7   Ibid.

Moritz Waldemeyer

1   J. McGuirk et al, 'The Icon 20/20 Designers: 6–10', *Icon*, 71,
    May 2009, p.85; N. Silver, 'The Electric Kid', *Metropolis*,
    December 2006.

2   A. Limnander, 'Star Tech', *New York Times, T Magazine*,
    1 April 2007.

3   J. McGuirk, 'The Lie Detector Test: Moritz Waldemeyer',
    Icon, 70, April 2009, p.69.

4   L. Fulton, 'Electro-luxe', *Grafik, Special Report Fashion*,
    April 2008, pp.56–61.

Simon Heijdens

1   Simon Heijdens, quoted in M. Belponti, 'Biography of Objects:
    Simon Heijdens', *Domus*, 876, December 2004, p.110.

2   I. Barros, 'Time Traffic: Simon Heijdens, Tension and
    Ability', *Dam*, December 2008, p.114.

3   J. Bell, 'Inside Out', *Grafik*, special report, 2007, p.71.

4   J. Blackburn, 'A Kinetic Aesthetic', 14 June 2008, FT.com,
    accessed 2 December 2010.

5   Ibid.

6   G. Perec, *Species of Spaces*, 1974, cited in Belponti 2004, p.109.

7   M. Kokhuis, 'A Warm Welcome', *Frame*, January/February
    2009, p.148.

Onkar Kular and Noam Toran

1   A. Dunne, 'One Million Little Utopias', in O. Kular,
    Accept No Other Imitations, 2009, p.31.

2   Kular 2009, p.3.

3   P. Jahn, 'Interview with Noam Toran and Onkar Kular',
    4 September 2008, http://www.electricsheepmagazine.co.uk/
    features/2008/09/04/the-macguffin-library, accessed
    21 July 2011.

4   Ibid.

5   O. Wainwright, 'Interview with Onkar Kular and Noam
    Toran', *Icon*, 88, October 2010, p.155.

6   *I Cling To Virtue*, exhib. cat., Victoria and Albert Museum,
    London, 2010.

Julia Lohmann

1   Julia Lohmann, quoted in A. Bates, 'The Lasting Void',
    Icon, 51, September 2007, p.38.

2   Julia Lohmann, quoted in J. Sims, 'A Beastly Business',
    The Independent, Extra supplement, 21 September 2006, p.23.

Glithero

1   Glithero, 'Manifesto', in *Miracle Machines and the
    Lost Industries*, self-published book, 2007.

2   http://www.studioglithero.com/index.php?/projects/running-
    mould---new, accessed 19 April 2011.

3   Glithero quoted in R. Etherington, 'The Long Drop by Studio

Glithero', http://www.dezeen.com/2009/09/27/the-long-drop-
by-studio-glithero/, 27 September 2009.

Martino Gamper

1   E. King, 'Biography of Martino Gamper',
    www.gampermartino.com, accessed 10 December 2010.

2   E. King, 'Ways of Sitting', in *What Martino Gamper did
    between two-thousand and two-thousand&four*, 2004, p.A.6.

3   Martino Gamper, quoted in 'Best of 2007', *Financial Times,
    House & Home*, 12 January 2008 (citing 'Best of 2007 feature,
    *Wallpaper** February 2008).

4   C. Brändle, 'Interview with Martino Gamper', in *Wouldn't
    it be Nice… Wishful Thinking in Art and Design*, exhib. cat.,
    Geneva 2008, p.209.

5   King 2004, p.A.6.

6   Martino Gamper, quoted in J. McGuirk, 'Martino Gamper
    100 Chairs 100 Days', *Icon*, 45, March 2007, p.58.

7   Martino Gamper, quoted in 'Best of 2007' 2008.

8   A. Stavrakos, 'Interview with Martino Gamper', *Bedeutung*,
    2, 2008, pp.96–109.

9   Martino Gamper, quoted in McGuirk 2007, p.60.

10 Martino Gamper, quoted in Brändle 2008, p.202.

11 Martino Gamper, quoted in J. McGuirk, 'Martino Gamper's
    Total Trattoria', *Icon*, 59, May 2008.

12 Martino Gamper, quoted in F. Rattray, 'Martino Gamper',
    i-D Magazine, 14 May 2008.

13 Martino Gamper, quoted in N. Swengley, 'There's a Sense
    of Freedom', *Financial Times, House & Home*, 6 June 2009.

Paul Cocksedge

1   'How We Met: Paul Cocksedge & Ron Arad', *The Independent*,
    6 May 2007, www.independent.co.uk, accessed 25 October 2010.

2   W. Shaw, 'Paul Cocksedge interview for London Design
    Festival 2010', www.londondesignfestival.com/editorials/
    paul-cocksedge-interview, accessed 25 October 2010.

3   Designmuseum.org/design/paul-cocksedge, accessed
    15 November 2010.

4   Shaw 2010.

5   'Introducing… Paul Cocksedge', *Evening Standard, ES
    Magazine*, 29 May 2009, www.thisislondon.co.uk, accessed
    25 October 2010.

6   Shaw 2010.

Committee

1   V. Richardson, 'Committee Deptford', *Blueprint*, 283,
    October 2009, p.53.

2   F. McAuslen, 'London Design Festival People', 17 September
    2007, www.timeout.com/london/aroundtown/features/3498/
    London_Design_Festival_people.html, accessed 10 January 2011.

3   www.designmuseum.org/design/committee, 2006, accessed
    29 November 2010.

4   Richardson 2009, p.53.

5   http://www.gallop.co.uk/flytip-wallpaper.htm#, accessed
    6 July 2011.

6   'Questions from Lladro', www.gallop.co.uk/porcelain, accessed
    19 December 2010.

7   http://www.gallop.co.uk/the-plastic-fandangos.htm#.

8   http://www.gallop.co.uk/lost-twin-ornaments.htm#.

400 601

Author's acknowledgements

Firstly, I would like to thank all the featured designers for their co-operation with this project. Thanks are also due to the Design Products Programme at the Royal College of Art, especially Hilary French and Tord Boontje, whom I also thank for his foreword. The RCA Research Office generously supported me with time and funding. Many thanks to Zofia Trofas and Rachael Crabtree for their efficient research, which made this book possible, Petr Krejčí for his wonderful and insightful portrait photography, Christopher Wilk for his constructive comments on the manuscript, A Practice for Everyday Life for a beautiful book design, Kate Bell for her editing, and Clare Davis, Mark Eastment, Kate Phillimore and Tom Windross at V&A Publishing.

Lastly, many thanks to Richard Sorger for bearing with me through another book.